Celebrating the 200th Anniversary
Of the Circus in America

1793-1993

AMERICA'S GREAT CIRCUS PARADE

Its roots...its revival...its revelry.

By C.P. "Chappie" Fox

AMERICA'S GREAT CIRCUS PARADE

Editor: Thomas Bell
Art Director: Janet Thalken
Art Assistant: Ellen Lloyd
Photo Coordination: Trudi Bellin

©1993, Reiman Publications, L.P.
5400 S. 60th St., Greendale WI 53129

International Standard Book
Number: 0-89821-111-5
Library of Congress
Catalog Card Number: 93-84887

Back cover photo by Brian Malloy

Acknowledgements

The Great Circus Parade, Inc., its officers, trustees and the author thank all the talented photographers whose work is included in this civic effort.

All photos are credited to the photographer where known.

We thank all of you for sharing your memorable and colorful work with the community so that the Great Circus Parade—Wisconsin's National Treasure—can be properly and beautifully recorded for all time to come.

And we are grateful to Kenneth Feld, President of Ringling Bros. and Barnum & Bailey Combined Shows Inc., for loaning the Circus World Museum four glorious, historic parade wagons that are used in the Great Circus Parade. These are the Ringling Bros. Bell Wagon, two beautiful tableau wagons from the old Hagenbeck-Wallace Circus and a Ringling Bros. pigmy hippo cage wagon.

And we thank Ringling Bros. and Barnum & Bailey Combined Shows for allowing us to reproduce the posters which carry a name they own and have trademarked.

We also thank John Zwiefel of Orlando, Florida for making available to the Great Circus Parade the huge Two-Hemispheres Bandwagon, which he owns.

Special thanks to Joe Weinfurter, Ben Barkin's able assistant. The myriad of details involved in putting this book together were handled with great dispatch by Joe.

The publication of this book added extra burdens on the office staff, and we thank Phyllis Thompson, Jean Herman, Wendy Porterfield and Virginia Kiekhaefer for their cooperation.

Mission Statement

THE GREAT CIRCUS PARADE, INC.

The mission of the Great Circus Parade, Inc. is to produce annually in the City of Milwaukee, Wisconsin an authentic re-creation of circus street processionals of bygone years.

In fulfilling this mission, it is the avowed intention of the Great Circus Parade, Inc., in cooperation with the Circus World Museum of Baraboo, Wisconsin, to raise the required funds in order to produce a unique spectacle that cannot be duplicated anywhere else in the world.

In addition to bringing joy to children of all ages around the world, the Great Circus Parade hopes to focus the national and international spotlight on Milwaukee and Wisconsin, and the Circus World Museum, as tourism destinations second to none, and thereby enhance the reputation and economy of city and state.

It is also the intention of the Great Circus Parade, Inc. to seek funds from all possible sources, statewide and nationally, for an endowment foundation, thereby ensuring the future of the Great Circus Parade.

Contents

Dedication

Chappie, "Radcliffe" and Ben Barkin at the Great Circus Parade of 1992.

To Ben Barkin—the man who had the vision and imagination to see the potential of the Great Circus Parade when the idea was presented to him in 1962.

Ben nurtured the parade, promoted the parade, encouraged the Circus World Museum to enlarge the parade; and since 1985 has single-handedly raised over 1 million dollars each year to assure Milwaukee the pleasure of this unique event.

Ben Barkin was the cement that held it all together.

Prologue

The Right Place At the Right Time

The idea for a modern-day replay of the old-time circus street processions of wagons, animals and performers was presented to me one fall day in 1962 by C.P. "Chappie" Fox, a prominent circus historian who was director of the state-owned Circus World Museum in Baraboo, Wisconsin.

He felt such a parade would be wondrous entertainment that would help draw attention and support to the emerging 3-year-old museum.

How right he was. But first there was a little detail to be considered: the financial means to put on this rather ambitious undertaking. It would take a pretty decent six-figure sum to do it right, and that certainly wasn't in the museum's modest start-up budget.

So Chappie started calling on possible corporate sponsors. He got 12 polite turndowns before he came to see me as the public relations counsel to the Joseph Schlitz Brewing Company.

There wasn't anything unlucky about Chappie's 13th try.

He didn't have an elaborate presentation, just some old photos of past circus parades, but he did have conviction, plus an obvious knowledge and great love of anything even smacking of circus. Most importantly, he had the sensational old wagons that would provide historic authenticity.

I fell for it immediately. It was a natural. Pageantry, Americana, history, wholesome fun for the whole family. In fact, I could see such potential that I had to caution Chappie, who envisioned the event bringing thousands and thousands of people to Baraboo.

"If you do it in Baraboo," I told him, "you'll never be able to provide enough bathrooms."

I felt pretty certain that the appeal of a genuine, nostalgic circus parade would not be lost on my client, Robert A. Uihlein Jr., president and CEO of Schlitz. Especially so, since he was a great lover of horses, which would be a major parade attraction pulling the big circus wagons.

It took Bob Uihlein 20 minutes to make up his mind. He liked the idea. He liked Chappie.

"Let's go for it, Ben," he said.

The first re-creation of an old-time circus street parade like those of the early

---

"If you do it in Baraboo, you'll never be able to provide enough bathrooms."

1900s rolled though downtown Milwaukee on the Fourth of July 1963 as a part of Old Milwaukee Days, sponsored by Schlitz and presented by the Circus World Museum.

It was less than half the size of today's huge 2-hour spectacle, with about 25 wagons and a couple of hundred horses, but it attracted half a million spectators. We felt we had an annual hit on our hands!

And we did. The parade grew steadily in size as we tried to top each previous year with new wagons and new attractions. The crowds swelled to as many as 800,000, and soon, the Great Circus Parade was a national attraction. The press coverage, including two *Life* magazine spreads, was very gratifying.

And Chappie was also right about the boost the parade would give the museum. Attendance at Baraboo climbed steadily, and the facilities expanded.

The Schlitz Brewing Company continued to sponsor the parade on the Fourth of July annually from 1963 to 1973, with the exception of one year

when travel was dampened by civil unrest.

In 1984 I was named "Headliner of the Year" by the Milwaukee Press Club. In my acceptance speech, lauding Milwaukee and its future, I made a casual and brief remark that it would be good for the city if the Circus Parade returned.

It was as if I had set off a rocket. Both daily newspapers picked up on the statement and carried "bring back the parade" editorials. "Go for it, Ben," said one headline, reiterating the commission of Bob Uihlein 22 years earlier.

I was trapped, happily trapped. The rebirth of the parade became virtually a full-time pursuit for me. With a lot of help from many wonderful, public-spirited corporations, foundations and individuals, I was able to raise $750,000. Chappie's original dream was reborn in greater glory on July 14, 1985.

We've produced the parade every July since then, even though its annual budget is now more than doubled that of 1985, and we've formed the nonprofit Great Circus Parade, Inc. to make sure the wagons never stop rolling.

This, after all, is the event *Reader's Digest* called, "One of the most stupendous, most sensational, most dazzling spectacles in America," and *National Geographic Traveler* has labeled it "…a stupendous, splendiferous cavalcade: ITSELF, ITS ONLY PARALLEL."

The Great Circus Parade, Wisconsin's national treasure, truly is a marvelous and unique event that draws worldwide attention to our community and state. It just seems to get better every year.

Ben Barkin

(Ben Barkin, a Milwaukee businessman and civic leader, is the founding organizer and the permanent trustee of the Great Circus Parade, Inc., Milwaukee.)

THE APPEAL of the circus around the turn of the century was simply unparalleled, particularly in the hardworking rural areas. Without television, radio or even a playhouse, the circus often represented the only form of public entertainment for the entire year.

A HORSE-DRAWN milk wagon, (at center) was photographed by the author at 12 years old in 1925.

CIRCUSES RELIED on up to 300 draft horses to transport equipment and wagons from the railroad yard to the show grounds. Here the Ringling stock cars are being unloaded (1945).

The Day the Circus Came to Town

"HORSES, Horses, Crazy Over Horses" was the name of a tune that was quite popular many years ago. I guess it could have pertained to me, because I've always been crazy over horses, particularly draft horses and the wagons that they pulled. Even at the age of 2, my parents informed me later, I was asking Santa Claus for a toy wagon.

By the time I was 10 or 12 years old, in the 1920s, I had an Eastman Kodak Brownie 2A model camera. I began to photograph the various draft horses and wagons that were still commonly seen on the city streets delivering milk, coal, ice and even hauling dump wagons.

But the BIG DAY for me each summer was when a railroad circus came to town, featuring 200 or 300 dapple grey Percherons. Now that was a sight to see—and photograph!

I became enraptured in the whole operation, and soon my great love of horses evolved into an even greater love for the circus.

Kept Us in Suspense

As I remember it, the anticipation was almost too much to bear.

Two weeks before the circus arrived in our town, what had been drab barns, tired sheds and worn board fences were suddenly splashed with color. Wondrous posters of lions, horses and elephants could only mean one thing to a kid: *The circus was coming to town.*

Soon as we heard the news, the circus became the main topic of conversation among us kids. Day by day the excitement mounted. And when the circus train finally pulled into our little village, you could just feel a change come over the entire town.

Some downtown businesses would shut down altogether on parade day. Others might close a little early, taking "time out" to examine the spectacle, or chat about it with a passerby. Everyone, it seemed, was in light spirits, including parents, who would often allow chores and homework to be postponed for this special occasion.

First thing in the morning, the train was unloaded just outside of town. Scores of big draft horses were led from

---

"Between the circus train, the show grounds, and the parade, there was almost too much to see and do..."

---

the stock cars, then put together in teams to roll wagons off the flatcars.

Other horses were hitched in six- or eight horse teams to pull the massive wagons to the show grounds. Exotic animals emerged from still more cars.

"Heads up!" shouted a worker, and all of us moved aside to let a string of zebras and camels go by.

Between the circus train, the show grounds, and the parade, there was almost too much to see and do.

The cage wagons were usually rolled off to the side of the street, since they were not needed until later on. We ran to the brightly colored wagons and gathered 'round them for an up-close look.

Often, we'd jump back as a muffled roar came from within a closed, paneled cage! Intriguing odors came from the wagon, and it was fun to guess whether the mysterious box held leopards, tigers or maybe even hyenas.

Soon it was time to walk to the show grounds. By the time we got there, some of the smaller tents were already set up. Crowds gathered at the cook tent to

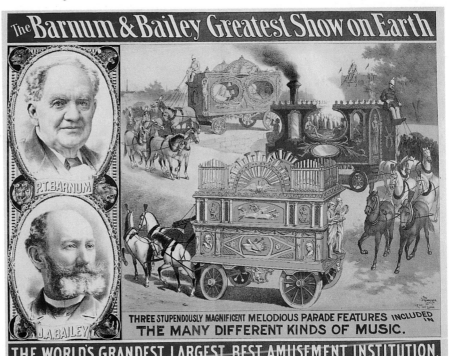

THE SHOWMEN had their advertising crew paste and hang hundreds of posters that illustrated their street parade and many of the beautiful wagons (circa 1890's).

watch the crew fry eggs and make pancakes by the hundreds for the hungry workers.

Everywhere we looked there was action—big teams of Percherons pulling heavy wagons...elephants in harness working hard...sweaty stake drivers pounding away. All of that activity was bewildering. But even though it was confusing to us kids, a circus setup was actually a highly organized process.

"Preview" Hyped Attendance

Once the main tent was set up and the seats and riggings were all in place, it was time for the street parade to wind its way through the heart of town and back to the show grounds, with children and adults following right behind it. It drew people like a magnet.

In my opinion, circus parades were the greatest, most alluring form of advertising ever conceived by man. If anyone had possibly forgotten when the

---

"Circus parades were the greatest, most alluring form of advertising ever conceived by man..."

---

circus was coming, well, once they saw and heard that parade, they knew exactly when and where it was, and what it featured.

Even those with a borderline interest became convinced that they just may have to attend after all. The sights, smells and sounds of the magnificent display were just too delightful for people to resist.

As advertising, the circus parade played on the three key senses: For the eye, there were stunning parade wagons, one after another, covered with intricate woodcarvings...lovely costumed girls riding handsome horses...and, of course, dozens of clowns, flags, ponies and banners.

For the ear, there was always a good number of bandwagons. The musicians played special instruments like unafones, band organs and bell wagons. A steam calliope brought up the rear and coaxed the crowd to the show like a Pied Piper.

Other sounds of the circus parade were the clip-clop of shod horses...the deep-throated knock of sunburst wheels ...the rattle of chains and the soft shuf-

TRADITIONALLY THE LAST UNIT in a circus parade, the steam calliope drew townspeople to the show grounds like a Pied Piper.

fling made by 30 or 40 passing elephants.

And the smells of the circus were like no other event. The aroma of the sweating horses combined with the exotic scents from the animal cages was a fragrance never to be forgotten. The circus parade was truly a feast for the eyes, ears and nose!

Time Ran Out for Parades

For decades through the late 1800s and early 1900s, these grand, free marches drew townsfolk to show grounds across America. But as the automobile gained popularity in the '20s, the appeal of the circus parade began to decline.

By 1940, its demise was complete. Heavier traffic—plus the stoplights that regulated it—forced circus parades off the streets.

Space and time were two more factors that hurt such parades. To be adequate, a show grounds had to cover nearly 10 acres. As urban sprawl pushed open spaces farther and farther from downtown areas, it made the parades so long they became impractical. There just wasn't enough time to take everything out on parade, and then get it all back to the grounds for the matinee.

And as time went on, draft horses, too, disappeared from the streets. I was

saddened by this turn of events, but I realized you cannot stop progress.

Reviving the Parade

However, because of my experiences with the circus, I was still hooked on this fascinating form of entertainment. So in the mid-1950s, I went to Baraboo, Wisconsin, the Ringling Brothers' hometown, to research a book I was compiling on the circus.

There I met John M. Kelley, an attorney who for 35 years had been the general counsel for the Ringling Brothers and their circus. I learned that day that John Kelley had been harboring a dream for many years—a dream to develop the Circus World Museum.

I was charmed into believing that this museum could be the greatest attraction in the state of Wisconsin.

As a result, it may not be surprising that I succumbed to an offer and took over the Directorship of the museum a

TAIL TRUNKING ELEPHANTS thread their way through throngs in Cleveland during the '20s. Below: The last of the big circus street parades, The Cole Bros. in 1939.

THE CREW of this 18-foot-long Ringling Bros. and Barnum & Bailey wagon are unloading equipment in Milwaukee in 1935.

drawn street parade.

Why I Wrote This Book

This book is sort of a "travelogue" which traces the fascinating route of my vision, and the steps, challenges and satisfactions I encountered along the way. It's the story of how that dream—with the help of many wonderful and generous people—eventually became a reality.

I guess I wrote this book for the same reason I wanted to start the parade back in 1963: My childhood fascination with the circus has never left me. I wanted to share that experience—the art, drama and history of those old circuses—with a new generation and put it in print before it's all forgotten.

few months after it opened its doors to the public.

Immediately, I found myself caught up in the excitement of collecting his-

toric horse-drawn wagons. And as these beautiful wagons began arriving at the museum, I started to envision the grand re-creation of an old-fashioned horse-

Maybe I needed to prove to myself that, although the times are changing, people are the same today as they were a hundred years ago. In short, they like to have fun.

Even today I have a kid's enthusiasm for the circus. When I hear there is a circus in the area, I never miss the opportunity to attend. And when the day of the Great Circus Parade rolls around every

> *"People are the same today as they were a hundred years ago. In short, they like to have fun..."*

July, I'm probably as excited as any kid in Milwaukee.

If you have ever had the opportunity to enjoy the Great Circus Parade over the years, I hope this book will rekindle some great memories and give you some background that will enhance those memories even more. If the Great Circus Parade is something new to you, I hope this book will help you feel you're "there", and maybe encourage you to attend in future years.

More than anything, I hope that as a result of reading this book, my enthusiasm for the Great Circus Parade proves contagious.

THE AUTHOR, C.P. Fox, tips his hat to the fans of the circus.

Celebrating 200 Years Of the Circus in America!

THE CIRCUS has stood the test of time—a good long time. A full 200 years ago this year, in 1793, an Englishman named John Bill Ricketts staged the very first American circus in Philadelphia.

Mainly an equestrian show featuring bareback riding and horse acrobatics, his circus also introduced a juggler, a clown, a band and even a rope-walker. A small, round wooden building paved the way for what would later become the big top.

Today, the tradition lives on—there are more than 40 existing circuses in America alone. This is quite remarkable when you think of all of today's competition out there for entertainment dollars…rock concerts, ice shows and motion pictures.

America has seen its share of changes in the last 200 years. But the tried-and-true, wholesome entertainment of the circus cannot be rivaled.

SPANNING THREE CENTURIES!

Above, the original promotion for John Bill Ricketts' 1793 circus. Above left, Sells Brothers' 1890 tour poster. Left, parading in Milwaukee, 1992.

Wisconsin was the home, birthplace and winter quarters of the Ringling Brothers and more than 100 other circuses during the 19th century. No other state has created as much circus fun.

★ Baraboo
Milwaukee ★

Pohlman Studios

A Preview Of Parade Week in Milwaukee...

THE Great Circus Parade in Milwaukee is an annual re-creation of the enticing street processions of wagons, animals and performers that traveling circuses of yesterday would stage upon their arrival in town to promote attendance.

Attractions of the Great Circus Parade include up to 60 historic circus wagons, several more than 100 years old. All resplendently restored by the craftsmen at the Circus World Museum, the wagons are the core of the big parade. This collection from the glorious heyday of the circus is unmatched anywhere on earth.

A clopping calvacade of more than 300 draft horses—part of a 700-plus equine ensemble from across the country—pulls the antique wagons over a 4-mile downtown route before hundreds of thousands of spectators.

Escorting the magnificent wagons are brassy bands, stirring military units, the shrill tones of the calliope, wild animals in caged wagons, scores of clowns and prancing riding horses.

The 2,000 costumed circus "performers", the fabulous 40-horse hitch and the largest herd of elephants in America collectively capture the essence of the circus. It's truly one of the greatest American forms of entertainment.

First presented from 1963 through 1973, then joyfully returning in 1985 after a 12-year hiatus, the Great Circus Parade continues to delight children of all ages from near and afar.

Crowd estimates have peaked at 1 million. Millions more view the nostalgic spectacle via some 200 public television stations coast to coast, and in more than 40 foreign countries across the globe including overseas U.S. military installations.

The Great Circus Parade is funded by contributions from public-spirited corporations, foundations and individuals. An endowment fund has been established so "Wisconsin's National Treasure" can continue to look forward to a future of bringing back the past.

The Great Circus Train and the Show Grounds

THE Great Circus Parade is actually the climax of a week-long series of events that makes Wisconsin the soul of the circus each summer.

A week before the parade begins, the wagons are loaded aboard railroad flatcars by horses, in the tradition of the circus, for the trip to Milwaukee.

That 2-day journey becomes a spectacle in itself as the train rolls leisurely through dozens of communities, with several stops, to give thousands of wagon watchers a close-up view of the priceless cargo of Americana.

At Milwaukee, the wagons and 700 horses and exotic circus animals are put on public display in a downtown Lake Michigan park as a part of a 4-day festival of circus entertainment that includes many free acts and daily big top circus performances.

Some special features unique to the '93 show grounds will include a 200th-anniversary display of circus memorabilia and a Grand Horse Fair exhibit of a dozen different breeds.

How It All Began...
Wisconsin's Great Circus Parade

When the Circus World Museum first opened its doors to the public on July 1, 1959, there were only a few historic circus wagons in the collection. I arrived in Baraboo 5 months later to take over the job of running the museum.

We were sort of Johnny-come-latelies in the museum business because there were already four circus museums in the United States. There were also organizations such as the Circus Fans Association of America, The Circus Historical Society and the Circus Model Builders Assn. Combined, they had a total of about 5,000 members. To varying degrees, these people are collectors of circus memorabilia; it is their pleasure, their hobby.

As Director of the Circus World Museum in Baraboo, I felt our primary effort should be to win the favor of these organizations. The key to that would be to concentrate on building up a wagon collection like no other.

After all, most circus buffs were busy collecting programs, photos, posters, etc. If we could collect historic circus wagons and circus railroad cars, I felt we could become a "mecca" to circus buffs around the world.

A big help to me was the fact that, back in 1953, I had published a book entitled "Circus Parades". It was a pictorial history of the old circus street parades. As a result of my research for this book, I knew the whereabouts of just about all of the old historic circus parade wagons.

No time was wasted in going "hammer and tongs" after these cherished relics. "You can't plow a field by turning it over in your mind—do it now," is one of my favorite maxims. So with this list as a starting point, the letters, phone calls, and personal visits began.

By 1961 and 1962, events began falling into place. With the help of people and organizations like Walt Disney and Universal Studios, we had obtained and restored about 30 wagons.

They were beautiful, and it seemed only natural that we should stage an old-fashioned circus parade to share these with more people. And if we did, it should be a parade the likes of which had not been seen in America since the '30s.

If it could be done, I felt this would be a sensational promotional stunt for the Circus World Museum, as well as for the town of Baraboo, and the state of Wisconsin as a whole. What's more, we could bring a piece of history back to life, and share a true, nostalgic circus experi-

Ron Brayer

ence with thousands of folks before this kind of event became a piece of the past.

But How to Cover Costs?

The need of a sponsor was quite obvious. To sell the idea, we needed a portfolio that would illustrate what a true circus parade was all about.

The museum was as poor as a church mouse, so to help tell our story, we settled for a few sheets of 8 x 11 planographs. The presentation was pitiful. But through friends in Milwaukee, I was able to get appointments with the top executives in some of Wisconsin's major corporations.

I received five or six very polite "This idea is interesting but it doesn't fit our company" responses. In other words, "No".

So I added a few more photos to my portfolio, selecting some showing the streets jammed with people watching a circus parade. Nevertheless, the seventh, eighth and ninth companies also said "No".

Number 10 showed a spark of interest. "We will give you $5,000 towards your goal of $42,000," they told me. Eleven and 12 joined the "No" crowd.

I wondered how all these intelligent executives could not see the potential in this idea. After all, if we could get the job done, the parade would be unique in all

---

> *"I told him we should reenact the parades of yesterday, and present everything just as it appeared at the turn of the century."*

---

the world. No one could copy it, as our museum possessed the last remaining historic circus parade wagons.

So I went to see Joe Johnson, president of the Milwaukee Company, an investment firm. Over lunch, he asked me how the parade idea was coming along.

I told him I had 12 turndowns and number 13 would be Schlitz. "Who are you going to see?" Joe asked. I told him I would try to see Bob Uihlein, the president of the company.

"You are making a mistake," Joe said, "You want to see Ben Barkin."

"Ben who?" I asked, exposing the fact that I was just a country bumpkin.

Joe continued, "Ben owns a public relations company here in town, and

Schlitz is one of his accounts. I think you would do better taking your idea to him. He's open to new ideas and knows what to do with them. When we get back to the office, I'll call him and see if he has time to see you."

Irish Luck was with me, as Ben was not only in his office, but he said for me to come right over. I was one nervous dude as I spread my pitiful portfolio before Ben and explained what the historic circus parades were all about. I showed him the 8x10 photos of the old-time parades.

Unlike the 12 others I'd shown them to, Ben's eyes sparkled, and I began to sense his interest.

I would say, "This photo was taken in Detroit, and this one in Cleveland." Ben would interrupt and say, "Do you mean these crowds jammed the streets to see a circus parade?" His interest was now turning into enthusiasm.

I assured him they did and told him why. I described the performers, the wild animals and the music, the beautiful horses and the colorful wardrobe.

I told him we should reenact the parades of yesterday, and present everything just as it had appeared at the turn of the century.

"Mr. Barkin," I said, "this kind of parade has everything. It is for people of all ages. It is for the family."

I could almost hear the wheels turning in his mind. He was seeing this exciting event being re-created. Good Lord, I thought, I have found what was missing in my 12 visits to other companies: *Vision.*

We talked on for quite a while, then Ben said, "You know, Chappie, this idea and this parade are too big for Baraboo. If the crowds are as immense as you say they will be, there won't be enough restrooms to handle everyone! If Schlitz is indeed interested, the Parade will have to be staged in Milwaukee."

Waiting for the Go-Ahead

When I finally left Ben's office he said, "Give me a couple of weeks and I'll get back to you." In the interim, I headed back and immediately began scouring the files for more old parade photos showing the crowds, now recognizing the impetus behind his interest.

When Ben's call finally came, he seemed delighted. I answered a slew of questions regarding the caged animals, horses, trucking the wagons and so forth. Then Ben said, "Come on over, we are going to the brewery to see Bob Uihlein."

BOB UIHLEIN (sponsor) and a tiger take some time to get to know each other.

Mr. Uihlein was very cordial and listened attentively as I explained my plans of a totally horse-drawn parade. He, too, asked about the wild animals and trucking the wagons. He said, "You say all the wagons will be drawn by six- and eight-horse hitches. Just where do you expect to find such teams in these modern times?"

"Mr. Uihlein," I responded, "I have had a deep interest in draft horses all of my life. I know who has big teams and, in fact, I have contacted enough of them already to know we can get the job done."

With that, Bob turned to Ben and said, "Let's go for it!"

Not 20 minutes had elapsed since we came into Mr. Uihlein's office. I could not believe it was true!

The Excitement Begins

Soon after Mr. Uihlein decided to sponsor the parade, I recall being asked to come to the brewery to explain the whole idea to a roomful of Schlitz executives.

I decided that if the huge crowds watching the circus parades of years ago were what caught Mr. Barkin's interest, then I would dwell on this point. I passed around my stack of old photos and explained what a circus parade was

PHOTOGRAPHS of enormous crowds such as the one below in New Orleans in the early '30s helped the author convince Schlitz to sponsor a circus parade.

all about. After all, I didn't believe anyone in the group had ever seen a real circus parade—they were too darn young.

I raved about the exciting music, the

"Bob Uihlein turned to Ben Barkin and said, 'Let's go for it.'"

---

beauty of the wardrobe and wagons, the cages of wild animals, the elephants, camels and hundreds of horses. I even expounded on the fascinating odors and the vibrant music, and why it all added up to such a spectacular event.

And then I pointed out that we had about 35 historic wagons; beautiful vehicles that were 80 and 90 years old. "The Circus Parade will be for children of all ages," I concluded.

Then Mr. Uihlein rose and spoke to his people. They are words that I will never forget.

"Let me remind all of you," he said, "Schlitz is going to sponsor this circus parade because it is a historic presentation. We are doing this as a corporate-level civic gesture for all of Milwaukee. This parade cannot be construed as an advertising stunt."

From the beginning, I had always emphasized that the parade should not be used to advertise a product. I was proud

BEN BARKIN sports his natural flair for public relations with a future parade participant.

to learn that Schlitz shared my sentiments. Never once in the 11 years of sponsorship did Schlitz ever renege on that commitment. Never, ever was a beer sign evident at one of the parades.

Thinking about the 13 contacts I made to find a sponsor, I came to the conclusion that 11 corporations had 0% vision; one had 10% vision; and Ben Barkin and Schlitz had 20-20 vision.

From Setbacks to Solutions

Parading in Milwaukee rather than Baraboo presented a whole new series of problems. Getting all of the wagons to Milwaukee and back meant a good deal of trucking. (Remember, the Circus Train

wasn't established until 1965.)

This was worked out with great dispatch by the Museum's next-door neighbor, Ed O'Brien, who owned and operated the Fullmer Trucking Co. In addition, Wilbur and David Deppe, with their array of lowboys and flatbeds, got involved.

Underpasses were checked for height, permits were obtained from the Department of Transportation and arrangements were made with the State Patrol to escort our trucks, which were to travel in a convoy.

When the convoy arrived in Milwaukee that first year in 1963, it was quite a spectacle. We were escorted right down Wisconsin Avenue with sirens screaming and all the truck horns blasting as we moved through red lights without even pausing.

Busy Milwaukeeans stopped whatever they were doing to cheer and whistle their greeting. Ben Barkin's publicity crew had been hard at work. And this "preview" of the parade did exactly what those parades through town did for those early circuses—it whetted people's appetites, got them talking about it and made it hard for them to resist attending.

Some Humble Beginnings

As we look at the assembly area used by the parade of today—a magnificent 15- to 20-acre level and grassed area of Veterans Park, along the shores of Lake Michigan, provided by Milwaukee County—I think back to that first assembly area we used in 1963.

It was at the lower end of a narrow street (North Jefferson Street) where there was a vacant lot off to one side.

This is where we parked the Ringling elephants and switched the Ringling cats to our historic cage wagons.

What's more, Walter Tacke, the head of Milwaukee's Department of Public Works, required us to put short pieces of 2-inch x 8-inch wood planks under the wagon wheels—he didn't want these heavy vehicles sinking into the pavement. He was thinking back 40 years when, on a hot August day, a steel-tired wheel on a horse-drawn wagon could sink into the warm asphalt. (So would the high heels of women's shoes for that matter.)

Actually, it was this very type of damage to the streets that was one of the factors that contributed to the death of circus parades in the '30s. However, what Walter had overlooked is that by 1963 the streets were paved with maca-

TRUCKING CONVOY rolling toward Milwaukee whetted appetites as it previewed the parade from the flatbeds.

dam, and the stones mixed with asphalt stabilized the surface so there was no problem at all.

As I'd guessed, the wheels of the wagons did no damage to Jefferson Street, or any other street on the parade route. In later years, when it came time to reminisce, Walter and I always had a good laugh about those blocks he'd had us place under the wheels that first year.

Concerned About Low Wires

On one of my trips to the Milwaukee Public Works Commissioner's Office that first year, I found that the city regulations required that all wires of any kind that were strung over the street had to be at least 18 feet above the pavement.

Since we had three or four wagons that towered up to 17-1/2 feet, I got to worrying about this. Sure, the law said 18 feet, but suppose a wire sagged. Or, suppose someone was hanging an advertising banner. Or, for some reason, we confronted a temporary wire that was less than 18 feet.

If any of those things happened, we could be in serious trouble during the parade. So, as a matter of course, that first year and each year after that, about a month before the parade, I would take fishing poles and tape them together to measure exactly 18 feet.

A police officer always accompanied us as we measured each and every overhead wire along the parade route. We must have got a lot of strange looks: A couple of guys walking down the middle of the street with an 18-foot fishing pole, but we had to do it.

And it was worth doing. Each year we found three or four wires that had sagged, and found some unauthorized wires that were as low as 14 or 15 feet.

They would have caused trouble. The top of the head of our "Statue of Liberty Girl", for example, was 17-1/2 feet from the pavement. These low wires were always reported and adjusted to proper height by parade time.

One year as we were starting out our measurements with that fishing pole, Paul Hayes, a reporter for *The Milwaukee Journal*, showed up. He trailed along watching our efforts. The next day his story explained what he perceived to be a fishing expedition. The fish poles were there and somehow he brought my felt hat into the story.

I don't go fishing, but I presume fishermen wear battered and worn-out hats—more power to them. But after I read Paul's story I looked my fedora over

COLLEEN BARNHART, "The Statue of Liberty Girl" towered 17-1/2 feet above the pavement.

That 'battered old hat'

"ARE you the reporter who said I came to town with a beat-up old felt hat?" Chappie Fox asked me recently. "I've had to live with that ever since. Even if I put on a hat that's never been worn, radio and TV announcers and newspaper reporters still describe me as wearing a beat-up old felt hat."

Is Fox imagining almost 25 years of hat abuse or is it true? The Milwaukee Journal and Milwaukee Sentinel archives were revealing.

I first referred to Chappie Fox wearing a "battered hat" in a June 5, 1966, story.

On June 29, 1969, another Journal reporter called it "his wretched, dusty, worn-out felt hat." On July 5, 1969, the Sentinel called it a "floppy old fedora."

On May 8, 1972: The Sentinel called it a "battered old chapeau," and, in September that year, "a battered brown felt hat."

In 1978. the Sentinel called it an "old felt hat" and, in 1983, simply a "brown fedora."

On July 5, 1985, the Sentinel again referred to it as "an old beat-up brown felt hat." Two days later, The Journal called it "a battered brown fedora."

The Sentinel was the newspaper that took outrageous liberty by assuming, in a 1972 story, that the fabled hat, or chapeau, was the source of Chappie's nickname. But The Journal started all the references to the "battered hat."

"I guess I kind of enjoy it," Fox said.

–P.G.H.

and I must admit it was a mess—stained ribbon, a hole in the peak and more than a little dusty.

So I took the hint and went over to the Donges Hat Store on Third & State Streets and bought two new Borsalinos. I felt right snappy. But the die was cast. No matter what kind of a hat I wore, brand-new or a few months old, all reporters, not just Paul, always referred to my beat-up hat. I couldn't win.

I remember P.T. Barnum was once quoted as saying, "There is no such thing as bad publicity", referring to his circus, of course. My consolation is, that every time my hat got into the act, no matter how it was described, either the parade or the Circus World Museum was mentioned, and that's good publicity.

So I can live with the battered hat syndrome—what the heck, you can't beat fun!

What About Grated Bridges?

We all learned to be prepared for anything. Startling developments could arise from just one phone call.

For example, one fall day I answered the phone and it was Milwaukee's Public works Commissioner telling me they were going to be replacing the planking on the State Street bridge with open steel grating surface. "Don't worry," he said, "the work will all be done by parade time."

Don't worry? Baloney! I immediately recalled the time in 1958 when the Cristiani Bros. Circus was in Milwaukee. The circus men had an extremely difficult time getting the elephants to walk across the open grating of the Wisconsin Avenue bridge. Horses acted the same way. They could see right through the grates down to the river, and they were reluctant to cross.

I thought about the draft horses, shod with steel shoes, and how dangerously slippery that could be. Then, too, we had ponies in the parade, and I wondered if their tiny hooves could get caught in the open grating.

I knew we had to find an answer. I put in a call to my good friend, Dr. J.Y. Henderson, the veterinarian for Ringling Bros. and Barnum & Bailey Circus. He told me about a rubber matting the circus industry uses when they perform so the horses won't slip.

On my next trip to Milwaukee I stopped in to see the Commissioner to explain my problem. The men in the Street Department were understanding. We got the specifications and ordered

LOADING UP in Baraboo for the first trip to Milwaukee in 1963.

TODAY'S assembly area and show grounds in Veterans Park on Milwaukee's lakefront.

geri, Billie Black (Ben's loyal secretary), John Baker, Don Dooley, Sarah Kimball and Phylis Thompson.

"But Which Way Do I Go?"

Early in the afternoon of July 4th, 1963, the very first Circus Parade was nearly under way. We brought the Ringling Bros. and Barnum & Bailey Circus to Milwaukee to augment our parade.

All of their elephants, big cats, camels and many performers were lined up and ready to go. The wagons and teams spanned both sides of Jefferson Street in their proper order. No detail had been overlooked.

I was standing next to the Introductory Wagon with four beautiful black Percherons. Ray Bast, President of the Percheron Horse Association of America, was holding the reins. He was an expert, and we knew we could depend on him.

I looked at my watch. It was 2 p.m. "Let 'er go, Ray!" I called. Ray looked down at me and said, "Chap, where do I go?"

In all the excitement, I had overlooked the most important detail of all—going over the route with the guy driving the lead wagon! Instant action was required because it was now 2:01, and I could feel a thousand eyes upon me.

"The crowds are lined up on both sides of the route, so just go between

the matting from Goodyear Rubber Co. A special wagon was prepared to haul these sheets of matting to the bridge on parade day. The men laid the heavy-duty rubber matting in place, and the entire parade passed without any difficulties.

A couple of years later a second bridge surface was changed to open grating, and we simply repeated the whole process.

The People That Made Her Sail

When we organized the very first Circus Parade, we were sailing in uncharted waters. Our naiveness was lessened, to a great degree, with some tremendous cooperation from the Milwaukee Police Department, Water Department, Street Department, the Fire Department, the Barkin-Herman and Associates crew and Milwaukee County officials.

I was also fortunate to get as volunteers Wally Lomoe, retired Managing Editor of *The Milwaukee Journal*; Duke Shumow, a Milwaukee businessman; Paul Ingrassia, a Rockford, Illinois businessman; and John Boyle from Cleveland, Ohio.

I had known all four of these capable men for many years and they were fascinated by the circus environment. They had the common sense and savvy to handle the myriad of questions and problems that came up during the course of the day.

In addition, dozens of volunteer circus fans from all over the U.S. helped with a thousand chores. These circus buffs who come each year to help with the last-minute details are invaluable. They come from all walks of life. We

have bankers, truck drivers, butchers, priests, welders and nurses—they all pitch in, and we need and appreciate every one of them.

In these early days, Ben's company (Barkin-Herman and Associates) did a splendid job of handling the many tasks involving the county and city departments and publicity.

Dave Herman, Ben's partner, was deeply involved, as well as Jean Herman, Joe Weinfurter, Jack Varick, Bob Rug-

the people," I shouted up to Ray. He whistled to his Percherons and off went the first parade.

After the entire parade was out on the street I sat on a bale of hay, worrying a little as I waited for it to come back to the assembly point. Finally, Ray Bast's team came into view.

When he reached me he called down, "It worked! I see what you mean."

The crowds were so enormous that there was no way he could have made a wrong turn.

Undertaker Among Volunteers

One of the early volunteers was Jim Moran, an undertaker who owned a large funeral parlor in Decatur, Illinois. Jim was assigned to the Wardrobe Department. On the morning of parade day, the Governor of Wisconsin arrived for his proper wardrobe—a turn-of-the-century outfit.

The Governor could not figure out how to tie his bow tie. His aide tried and failed. Finally, the aide called out, "Does anyone know how to tie a bow tie?"

Jim Moran overheard the question and said, "Ask the Governor to lay down on a table and I will tie it for him!"

Another thing we always had to be concerned about on parade day was the

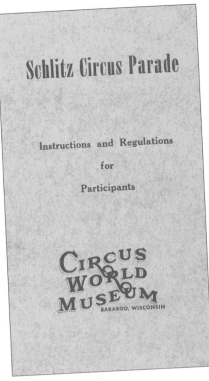

Schlitz Circus Parade

Instructions and Regulations

for

Participants

CIRCUS
WORLD
MUSEUM
BARABOO, WISCONSIN

moods of all the animals.

For example, we learned that a cage full of tigers next to a six-horse team could spell trouble. The exotic odors of elephants, camels and the big cats tend

to make a horse jumpy and nervous.

To prevent this, we suggested to the drivers of teams that they rub just a bit of mentholatum, or Vicks, on the noses of their horses to ward off these unfamiliar smells.

Frank Rossler drove a beautiful six-horse team of Belgians. On parade day one year, while he was hitching up to his assigned wagon, he turned to his wife, Mabel, and said, "Did you bring the mentholatum?" Mabel had forgotten this chore and there wasn't time to go back to the horse tent to get it.

So Mabel, being a real trooper, opened her purse and produced a cherished bottle of perfume. She emptied it on her handkerchief, then swabbed a bit on the noses of all six Belgians.

This maneuver worked, but it didn't convince us to change the rules in our published booklet of instructions and regulations.

This was an interesting pocket-sized booklet with special information for the parade participants. Safety was always our top priority.

The booklet contained answers to all questions and had been mailed in advance to each participant. It listed precautions, instructions for outriders, such as "no stallions", no "hot horses" and no kids as "joy riders". It also covered Riding Troupes, Marching Bands, Clowns, Top Riders and Volunteer Workers.

For the horses and ponies, the booklet let horse owners know that we would furnish hay and bedding. It also informed them that we had installed picket lines in all tents and piped in fresh water to tanks. Plus, it informed them that we had a farrier and a veterinarian available on the show grounds.

A Touching Story

To me, there is one particular episode during these early years of the parade that was both touching, delightful and gratifying. It made all of my hard work pay off in an instant.

John M. Kelley, an attorney from Baraboo, was the Founder of the Circus World Museum. It was he who came up with the idea, thought up its name and incorporated it.

When he first talked up the idea, people snickered about John Kelley's dream. But he stuck to his guns.

In that first parade, John was to have the privilege of riding in the lead carriage with Bob Uihlein and his wife. When the carriage arrived and pulled over to the

JOHN KELLEY, Founder of the Circus World Museum, lived to ride in the lead carriage of the first Great Circus Parade.

curb in front of me, a man looking 90 years old popped out.

Dressed in turn-of-the-century clothes, top hat and all, he walked over to me with long, proud strides. His gangly arms swung up and his hands landed on my shoulder.

He looked me straight in the eye and said, "Now, by God, people will know there is a Circus World Museum in Baraboo!" It was then I realized it was John Kelley, in a fitting costume!

Six months later, John Kelley passed away. I thank the Lord he had the satisfaction of riding in that first parade.

Calliope Left Behind

Harry Heck, a man from Illinois known for his horsemanship, had always been featured in our parade with his beautiful team of eight Belgians. Over the years Harry kept asking to drive the America Steam Calliope Wagon, the unit that is traditionally the last in every circus parade.

Eventually the opportunity arose, and I called Harry. He was extremely pleased. I reminded him that this wagon was enormous—it weighed 9 tons with a full tank of water and a full tank of oil. Harry assured me he and his team could handle it.

On parade day Harry was hitched and ready to go. He had purchased brand-new sets of harness especially for the parade with beautiful black leather and chrome-plated hardware. The procession was already gliding through Milwaukee's streets, with everything going as planned.

Harry pulled up to the spot where he would move out, just behind the ele-

---

" 'A hame strap broke!' he moaned..."

---

phants. I looked up at Harry and waved him into the march. Harry whistled, and his eight massive Belgians leaned into their collars. The 9-ton load began to roll.

Then it happened. A key hame strap broke on one of the wheel horse's harness. Harry handed the lines to his brake man and was off that 10-foot-high perch in a flash.

A couple of his outriders came back to the wagon. Harry spoke a few quick words, and an assistant galloped off toward the horse tent.

I walked over and Harry showed me the trouble. "A brand-new expensive

THE AMERICA Steam Calliope weighs a solid 9 tons. Played like a piano, when a key is depressed, pressurized steam shoots through a series of whistles. The rousing music can be heard for 5 miles.

harness," he moaned, "and a hame strap broke!" (Hame straps are a very critical part of any harness.) "My outrider will be back in a minute."

The minute extended into 5 minutes. "Harry," I said, "you will have to give up on the parade. You can never catch up. Those city street sweepers will fall in behind the elephants when they see no calliope in sight. Furthermore, the streets will be jammed with people. You will never be able to get through the crowd!"

It was a tough decision for me to have to make. And it was a tough decision for Harry to swallow. We both felt bad about it.

Some years later our paths crossed in Florida. I was with Ringling Bros. and Harry was driving the eight Budweiser Clydesdales for Anheuser-Busch. Naturally, we reminisced and, in effect, cried on each other's shoulders.

"When that hame strap broke, it was the worst moment in my life," Harry said.

"Mine, too, Harry," I replied.

The Police Were Just Great

The Police Department always posi-

tioned a trailer on the show grounds for their Command Center. Lt. Busalachi was in charge of it.

Each morning I spent 15 or 20 minutes with him discussing things in general. At one of these sessions, the Lieutenant commented that the entire Police Department enjoyed working when the Circus Parade came to town, because everyone was happy—no pushing, no shoving and smiles all around.

The men in our work crew always made it a point to get involved with the officers on duty. It gave our boys a good feeling that this special teamwork existed, and it reinforced a feeling of safety and thoroughness.

A couple of hours before the first parade began, I found myself stuck in a mob of people, desperate to get back to the show grounds before it all began. Traffic was terrible. I stood on the curb mumbling to myself because there wasn't a taxi in sight.

Then I heard a voice say, "What are you cussing about?" I turned around and there was the Chief of Police, Harold Breier. I told him my tale of woe and just at that moment the Chief's car arrived to pick him up. "Stop grumbling, Chap," he said. "Get in, I'll take you to the grounds."

The ride only took a couple of minutes, but it struck me that this feeling of teamwork—between our gang from the Circus World Museum and the Milwaukee Police Department—emanated from the top down. The Chief could not have been more pleasant and he surely was interested in the parade.

Harnessing Real Horsepower

The horses were an extremely important asset to the entire Parade effort—in fact, they were sort of its backbone. After all, it was draft horses that supplied the movement for the whole event.

John Barnhart from Baraboo was in charge of the horse tents. He not only knew horses, but he understood the people who brought the many teams. John spoke their language, and as a conse-quence, this department sailed along smoothly.

A sort of community developed around these "horse people". Many men and their families who owned horses, but were not Parade participants, showed up in Milwaukee just so they could be among their friends.

For the horsemen in the Parade, the event became an annual outing for the entire family. Each member had a chore —be it cleaning harness, feeding, water-ing or grooming.

We insisted that all teams arrive in Milwaukee early on Saturday before the parade, to hitch up and practice with their assigned wagon. We wanted the driver to get the feel of the load his horses were hauling, and the horses to get the feel of their new situation.

Many Marching Musicians

Frank Caveney organized all of the high school marching bands, and coor-dinated their participation. The Wardrobe Department produced a new wardrobe for the bands each year. The parade usu-ally featured eight or nine 100-piece bands, so that meant an awful lot of measuring, sewing and fitting.

One band was outfitted like the Royal Bengal Lancers, another wore Indian costumes. We had bands dressed in Chi-nese garb, clown garb and military wardrobe. One band wore white jackets and pants trimmed in gold and red. Another wore white pants and green jackets trimmed with silver.

We made it clear to all of the bands that the songs had to fit the era of the big circus street parades. We didn't want any fancy orchestrations, just good old-fashioned, lively marching music.

Each band was required to play a dif-ferent song. One would pick "Ringling Bros. Grant Entry", another "Billboard March", or "Barnum & Bailey's Favor-

BOB LUDWIG'S MOUNTED BAND was a sensation, but it was a trick—the horses had to get used to music blaring in their ears.

A GROUP OF DRIVERS AND THEIR TEAMS pose for a publicity photo. Belgians, Percherons and Clydesdales are all represented.

ite", for example. Knowing one tune was sufficient because marching bands are constantly playing in front of a new audience. And by *memorizing* one tune, the kids did not have to have music in front of them, which could be a pain in the neck on a windy day.

In real circus tradition, we had to have a mounted band. Bob Ludwig of Oconomowoc, Wisconsin agreed to teach his band to ride horses. (We figured that'd be easier than teaching 18 experienced horsemen to play instruments.)

Now this was a tricky deal. The horses had to get used to instruments blaring in their ears. The musicians learned quickly to turn their heads and instruments slightly to the right or left. This was done so that if a horse tossed its head up, we would not be left with a toothless musician.

Practice, practice and more practice did the

job…and it was worth it. Bob's band was a sensation. In the end, the music every year has been wonderful in contributing to the festive spirit of the parade.

An Incredible Success

Ben Barkin was quoted in *The Milwaukee Sentinel* as saying, "We were determined to give Milwaukee something unforgettable, but none of us dreamed how big this would turn out to be."

The first Circus Parade was now history, and a complete success. Be it the roar of the caged lions, the antics of a troupe of clowns or the elaborate antique wagons, there seemed to be something for everyone to enjoy.

We had succeeded in bringing back a tradition that was very special to early America. That being done, people weren't about to let it die again! Immediately, we found ourselves showered with requests for an encore. What could we do? You can't beat fun.

Year after year, we made it a point to push ourselves and ask the question, "What can we do to make the Circus Parade even better?"

Looking back to circus parades of years ago, we found exciting features that made the parade more colorful, unique and pleasing to the audience.

We made dozens of minor changes every year simply because we kept learning how to do things more efficiently.

Also, as more people found out about the parade, our budget got larger, and we could afford improvements. Some of them were:

1964—The new Wardrobe Department. This overhaul of costumes added a flash of color that came to define the parade.
1965—This was a banner year for the Circus Parade. Not only did we add the Circus Train, but Bob Parkinson came on board as my assistant and as the Director of the Circus Museum Library.
1968—The addition of the stunning English Parade Wagons.
1970—Ernie and Tova Borgnine joined the parade.

1972—Dick Sparrow and his 40-horse hitch joined the line-up.

The Fabulous 40-Horse Hitch

The 40-horse team was probably the most spectacular addition to the Great Circus Parade ever. However, it took a few years to materialize.

In the late 19th century, a number of circuses used a 40 to emphasize the enormity of their show. It hadn't been done since 1904, so I began dreaming about bringing back another lost art.

In the fall of 1968 Ben Barkin posed his usual question, "What's new for next year, Chappie?"

I suggested a 40-horse hitch. "Oh, no," was the answer. "We must always think of safety." So I let it drop, figuring we would have to work into this one slowly.

Dick Sparrow was one of our very best horsemen. Over the years in the parade he was hitching his Belgians four abreast without a problem. He was the man, I felt, who could handle the 40. So, for 1969, I said to Dick, "How about driving a 12, four abreast?"

He did it and it looked great.

In the spring of 1969 we had "Bob Uihlein Day" at the Circus World Museum. During the festivities Mr. Uihlein was presented with a 1/4-inch scale

---

"Nobody has driven a 40-horse hitch since 1904!"

---

model of the Two Hemispheres Bandwagon pulled by 40 horses. Mr. Uihlein kept this model on his desk at the Schlitz Brewery. I think we planted a seed.

The next year I suggested to Dick Sparrow that he go for 16 horses, four abreast. "Sure." He said. It looked beautiful. Then, in 1971, Dick drove a 20-horse hitch. We were getting close.

In the fall of 1971 Ben asked again, "What's new?" I said, "Ben, you know in the last Parade Dick drove a 20-horse team and it was spectacular. Let's go for 40. Just think of it. Nobody has driven a 40-horse hitch since 1904."

"Can Dick do it? Will it be absolutely safe? One man driving all those horses scares me," Ben countered.

A Tight Squeeze

You see, I had made the mistake of letting Ben read a book titled "The Last of the 40-Horse Drivers", by Jake Posey. Posey drove the Barnum & Bailey 40

AWARD-WINNING actor Ernest Borgnine and his wife, Tova, joined the parade in 1970.

while they were in England and Europe from 1898 through 1902.

In one chapter, the author explains an accident during a street parade. He had to turn into a street that was barely wide enough for the four abreast team.

As the wagon made the sharp, tight turn, the hub of the rear wheel caught the door of a pub called the "Flower Pot Inn". The hitch pulled out the entire front half of the pub! The circus squared the

---

"The circus repaid the damage with a fistful of tickets..."

---

damage with a fistful of free tickets, and the Flower Pot Inn changed its name to the "40-Horse Inn".

This incident stuck in Ben's mind. Not being familiar with horses, he simply could not understand how one man could drive 40 of them. And I didn't blame him, but Dick Sparrow wasn't just any horseman.

Finally, Ben agreed to set up a meeting with Bob Uihlein to discuss the idea.

Dick Sparrow and his wife, Joy, Ben Barkin, Bob Uihlein and myself met for lunch at the Milwaukee Club. The entire conversation was about horses. Then we discussed the 40.

After looking at a lot of old photos and listening to the conversations, Bob turned to me and said, "Do you really think it can be done?" My answer was, "Probably a dozen circuses have done it in the past, and I am confident that in Dick Sparrow, we have a man that can do the job safely."

Then Bob turned to Dick and asked, "Do you think you can do it, Dick?"

Dick said, "Mr. Uihlein, if it has been done before, I can do it. I can drive any team that any other man has."

Before Ben could open his mouth, Bob turned and said, "Well, Ben, it looks like you just lost. It's three to one."

So in the 1972 Great Circus Parade, Dick drove the 40. It was a flawless performance. The dramatic sight brought a standing ovation along the entire 3-1/2-mile parade route!

As it turned out, the 1972 Great Circus Parade was a very memorable occasion for me. After directing the Circus World Museum for the first 13 years of its existence, and organizing and directing the first 10 Circus Parades, I was giving up this very pleasant job.

Irvin Feld, President and owner of Ringling Bros. and Barnum & Bailey Circus, asked me to join his organization.

A Little Choked Up

Late in the afternoon the day before the parade, we always called all the horsemen together for a meeting to discuss any loose ends, answer any questions and wish them all the best of luck in the parade.

This being my last parade, after 10 beautiful years of working with these men and their families, I kind of got all choked up when they presented me with a wonderful album which contained a letter from each of the horsemen on their farm stationery.

Each man wrote a beautiful "thank you" note and pasted a photo of his team pulling a circus wagon in the parade on the letterhead.

I have received many fine gifts in my time, but none that I cherish as much as this album.

In all my years I have never met or worked with a finer bunch of people. The show grounds were like an unofficial family reunion. Everyone obeyed our regulations, cooperated and took pride in doing the best job possible. In my heart I hoped the Parade would go on forever.

I was saddened to hear, however, about a year later, that Schlitz, for many and varied reasons, gave up sponsorship of the Circus Parade.

There was a 12-year hiatus with no parade.

In 1983, after 12 years with Ringling, I retired and moved from Florida back to Baraboo.

Saluting Ben Barkin

I want to end this chapter by saying a word or two about my friend, Ben Barkin. It was his vision that others lacked that made him realize the potential of a historic circus parade.

It was his insight that very quickly understood the tremendous impact the addition of the Circus Train would have on the entire event. It was his savvy that caused him to say to me each year, "What's new?"

It was Ben's belief in the Great Circus Parade that brought it back to life in 1985, after a 12-year hiatus.

There were those pessimists who said, "Ben, you have shot your wad. It won't sail again."

Ben Barkin persisted, and his vision became reality. The Great Circus Parade was reborn in 1985, and has sailed annually ever since. Rain or shine, the

Great Circus Parade, Inc.

Great Circus Parade.

THIS DRAMATIC sight of the 40-horse hitch brought a standing ovation along the entire 3-1/2-mile parade route.

enthusiastic crowds are just as great as always.

There are those who will say, "But you had the idea for the Great Circus Parade…you thought up the Circus Train…you collected the wagons."

That is all true, but how far could the Circus World Museum, in little old Baraboo, carry our dreams without money? We would be dead in the water. We needed a catalyst like Ben Barkin who had two things: The vision to see the poten-

tial of a circus parade; and the ability to raise the necessary funds to stage the Great Circus Parade.

We in Baraboo have the bricks, but Ben Barkin is the mortar—the cement that has held the whole event together.

Parade Draws National Focus

The big circuses that moved from town to town by railroad flourished between 1880 and 1920. In a changing, uncertain era, the thrill of the circus was a much needed diversion. Competition was fierce between about 50 rival circuses—ensuring the public extraordinary productions that were constantly being upgraded.

The great lengths to which these circuses went to outdo

each other were most visible in their dazzling parades, which eventually became as much of an attraction as the circus itself. On the street, a circus had the opportunity to revel in its own extravagant glory and overwhelm its audience with blaring music, strange animals and exotic wagons.

When the Great Depression hit, however, the circus felt the crunch as much as anyone. Folks just didn't have the money to spend on entertainment. Several circuses continued to exist, meagerly, but their elaborate parades

LIFE

BOB KENNEDY'S WEEK OF TRIAL AND DECISION

A happy moment at home with his and his brother Jack's children

COURTNEY   KERRY   CAROLINE

THE GREAT CIRCUS PARADE began receiving attention from the national media almost immediately following its inception. The *Life* spread at right is from 1964, the parade's second year. The following pages highlight a handful of the over 200 magazines and newspapers that have covered the parade.

TURNER BROADCASTING CO. televised the Great Circus Parade in 1985. Above, Ted Turner, Ben Barkin and Chappie Fox. Each year, national magazines cover the parade. A few of these publications are shown here.

＊

were no longer practical.

In 1939, Americans witnessed what was thought to be the last horse-drawn circus parade ever. A unique and wonderful tradition appeared to be lost—a casualty of the changing times.

But in 1963, on the streets of Milwaukee, the historic circus parade was reborn!

With an arsenal of restored antique wagons, hundreds of volunteers from across the country and sponsorship from the Schlitz Brewery, the Circus World Museum resurrected a timeless celebration.

Why All the Publicity?

The public applauded its joyous return. And newspapers and magazines from all over the country were inspired, to say the least.

The first Great Circus Parade stirred memories in the minds of older members of the media. They realized that many of the parade's restored circus wagons may have been the very ones that rolled down the streets of their old hometowns, back when they were kids. They felt a sudden hankering to cover the event.

And every parade since ('93 will be the 19th) seems to generate more and more attention from the national media. By the '80s, newspapers from places as far away as Saudia Arabia and China were writing up the parade.

When the circus train eases into Milwaukee, the irresistible mixture of nostalgia and pageantry draws hundreds of admirers.

Photographers have a field day shooting what many have labeled "the most photogenic event ever". Capturing the dynamic colors and glimmering wardrobe of the gallant procession—with hundreds of horses, elephants, camels and wild animals—is an enviable task.

Feature writers revel in the wholesome entertainment the parade provides. There is something to engage the attention of every member of the family. And the smiling faces of more than 500,000 applauding spectators add more than a little "human interest" to the feature stories.

Much of the press, like the *Milwaukee Sentinel*, no doubt appreciates the "happy partnership between public and private enterprise" the parade represents,

"Rain or shine, between 500,000 and 800,000 people from all over the country line 3-1/2 miles of downtown Milwaukee every year..."

calling it, "Something all cities could use more of".

I think people like the fact that the

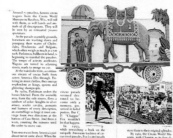

THE PARADE THAT'S MAKING MILWAUKEE FAMOUS

By Louis A. Goss

This spectacular event draws miles of smiles from young and old alike.

CHAPPIE MET VANNA WHITE (above) when she and Pat Sajak did the commentary for the nationally televised 1985 parade.

Great Circus Parade was not conceived as a publicity stint, and never has been. It is an authentic, historic reenactment. The parade is a tribute to America's heritage and a public service for the people of Wisconsin to enjoy.

What? No Dignitary?

The organizers of nearly every other parade carefully select a politician, celebrity or some other well-known person to head up their parade. Not the Great Circus Parade. "By the people, for the people" is one of our mottos. So it's only appropriate that "regular folks" be given key roles in this parade... including the role of Grand Marshall.

Shortly before the parade, the names of all the contributors (of $1 or more) are dumped into the "Old Woman That Lived in the Shoe" float. The person whose name is drawn becomes the Grand Marshall for that year's parade. It could be anyone!

In addition to the print media, local television stations throughout Wisconsin broadcast the Great Circus Parade live every year, and have since the very first reenactment in 1963.

PBS also covers the event, and sells its film to over 140 television stations in the United States and to a number of foreign outlets. American servicemen around the world view this broadcast via the Armed Service Satellite Network. Bob Keeshan ("Captain Kangaroo") does the announcing, and prominent circus historians add interesting facts and color to his narration.

Turner Broadcasting Co. of Atlanta nationally televised the parade in 1985. Pat Sajak and Vanna White provided the narration for the procession, and their playful commentary entertained people all over the country.

Still Amazed

When the Great Circus Parade was still in its planning stages, Ben Barkin and myself kept trying to predict how

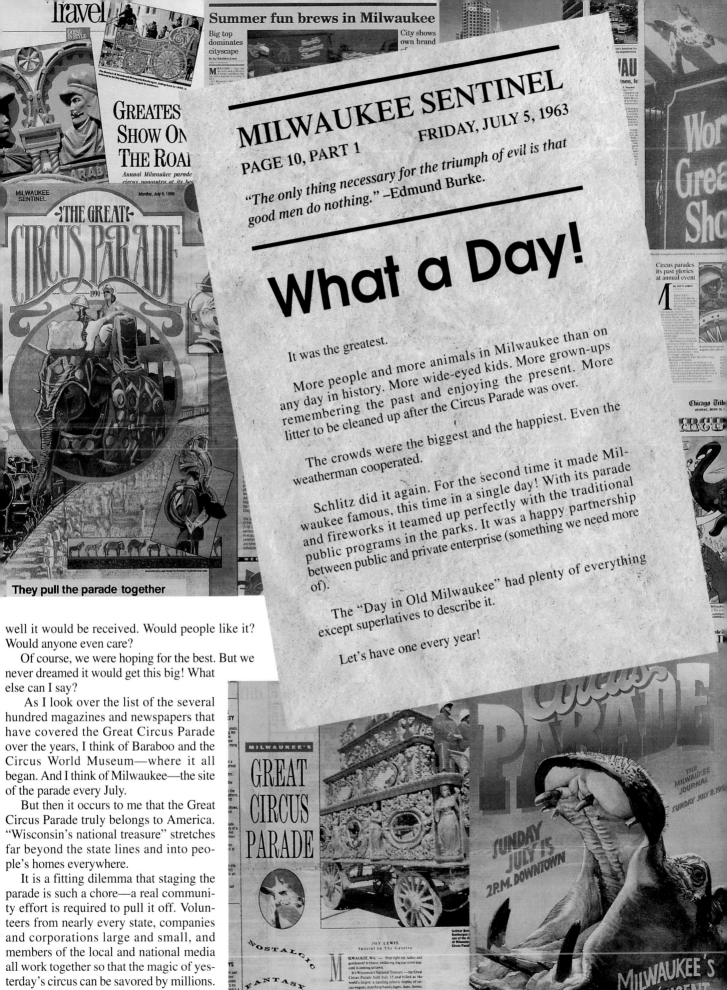

GREATES
SHOW ON
THE ROAI

Annual Milwaukee parade
circus pageantry at its bes

Summer fun brews in Milwaukee

Big top
dominates
cityscape

City shows
own brand

MILWAUKEE
SENTINEL

Monday, July 9, 1990

THE GREAT
CIRCUS PARADE
1990

They pull the parade together

Wor
Grea
Sho

Circus parades
its past glories
at annual event

Chicago Tribu

MILWAUKEE SENTINEL
FRIDAY, JULY 5, 1963
PAGE 10, PART 1

"The only thing necessary for the triumph of evil is that good men do nothing." –Edmund Burke.

What a Day!

It was the greatest.

More people and more animals in Milwaukee than on any day in history. More wide-eyed kids. More grown-ups remembering the past and enjoying the present. More litter to be cleaned up after the Circus Parade was over.

The crowds were the biggest and the happiest. Even the weatherman cooperated.

Schlitz did it again. For the second time it made Milwaukee famous, this time in a single day! With its parade and fireworks it teamed up perfectly with the traditional public programs in the parks. It was a happy partnership between public and private enterprise (something we need more of).

The "Day in Old Milwaukee" had plenty of everything except superlatives to describe it.

Let's have one every year!

well it would be received. Would people like it? Would anyone even care?

Of course, we were hoping for the best. But we never dreamed it would get this big! What else can I say?

As I look over the list of the several hundred magazines and newspapers that have covered the Great Circus Parade over the years, I think of Baraboo and the Circus World Museum—where it all began. And I think of Milwaukee—the site of the parade every July.

But then it occurs to me that the Great Circus Parade truly belongs to America. "Wisconsin's national treasure" stretches far beyond the state lines and into people's homes everywhere.

It is a fitting dilemma that staging the parade is such a chore—a real community effort is required to pull it off. Volunteers from nearly every state, companies and corporations large and small, and members of the local and national media all work together so that the magic of yesterday's circus can be savored by millions.

MILWAUKEE'S
GREAT
CIRCUS
PARADE

NOSTALGIC
FANTASY
IN SCARLET

JOY LEWIS
Special to The Gazette

CIRCUS
PARADE

SUNDAY
JULY 15
2 P.M. DOWNTOWN

THE
MILWAUKEE
JOURNAL
SUNDAY JULY 15

MILWAUKEE'S
MAGNIFICENT
MARVEL

SOUVENIR

The Evolution of a Painting

or, the appearance and disappearance of the picture plane

BY COLLEEN BROWNING

Step 1. The division of the canvas into the three fices of the wagon.

THE ROAR
OF THE CROWD

Hurry! Hurry! Hurry back to the golden age of the circus.

BY MARY-PAIGE ROYER

WILLARD SCOTT from NBC with Chappie.

Jim Morrill

A Peek into the
Past in Milwaukee

OLD-TIME
WAGO

AGAIN

Sunday **PICTURES!** ST. LOUIS POST-DISPATCH

US kids
A Weekly Reading Magazine

Vol. 2, No. 8
July-August 1989

RAILFAN RAILROAD

DECEMBER 1992 $2.95

Chicago Tribune Sunday Maga
JULY 2, 1967
h in Milwaukee Page 6 | Is July 4 Really

The Show Never Stops at The Circus World Museum

CHAPTER THREE

he Circus World Museum is an amazing yet complex operation. I know, because I ran it for 13 years—1959 through 1972. Things have a way of changing as time passes, so I have asked Greg Parkinson, the current Executive Director of the museum, to write a narrative about the institution he guides.

He was willing, and here is what Greg has to say about the place Ben Barkin refers to as "that gem in Baraboo":

For 200 years, the circus in America has captured the hearts of children of all ages with its pretty equestriennes, elephants and clowns.

Today, the Circus World Museum commemorates the star-spangled heritage of the circus ring on the banks of the Baraboo River, in south-central Wisconsin.

The Washington Post has proclaimed, "Every day is circus day at the Circus World Museum." *The Boston Globe* has

JORGE BARREDA and his African lions enthrall audiences beneath the museum's big top.

Ron Brayer

THE Irvin Feld Exhibit Hall and Visitor Center greets guests with an array of major displays, exhibits and artifacts. At left, a trio of lumbering elephants performs in the daily street parade.

Great Circu[...]

BOB UIHLEIN, former President of the Schlitz Brewery, purchased this collection of 3,300 original circus lithographs as a gift for the museum in 1967. This collection put the Circus World Museum Library in a second-to-none category in the world.

referred to it as, "The most exciting, noisy and color-splashed museum you will ever see." *The Des Moines Register* calls it, "A big dose of Americana and family fun."

This joyous institution, where the magic of yesterday's circus comes to life, is all of this, and much, much more.

Loads of Learning

To fulfill its mission, the museum offers a kaleidoscopic array of demonstrations, educational exhibits and action-packed shows.

Upon entering Circus World, visitors first see the Irvin Feld Exhibit Hall and Visitor Center. This is a gigantic brick structure housing state-of-the-art exhibits, including "The Art of the American Circus", a glittering display of circus "spec" artifacts, plus original costumes, floats and lithographs.

Guests are also entertained and informed in a modern 100-seat theater. A wide-screen presentation about the legendary circus superstar Gunther Gebel-Williams—and his unbelievable rapport with tigers, elephants and horses—fascinates audiences every half hour.

Train loading shows utilize original circus equipment and Percheron draft horses to load and unload railroad flatcars, employing the same system pioneered by one of P.T. Barnum's original partners, W.C. Coup.

Horse-drawn circus street parades (small by comparison to the Great Circus Parade), are presented each day throughout the summer season, from May through August. Antique bandwagons, cages and calliopes along with horses, ponies, elephants, camels, acrobats and cavorting clowns stroll joyfully through

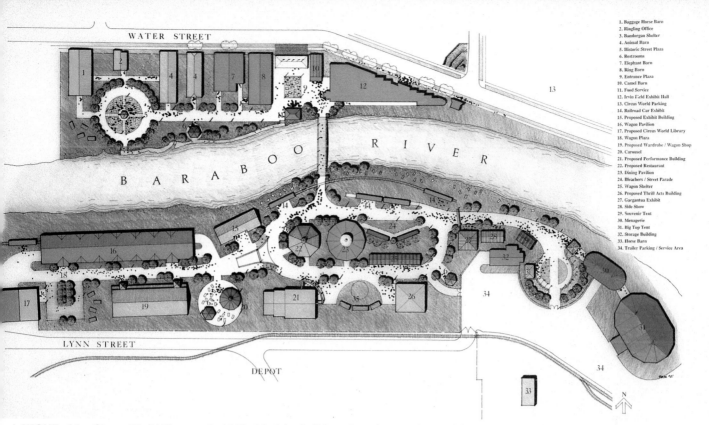

BARABOO RIVER

LYNN STREET

DEPOT

LAYOUT of the Circus World Museum in 1992. All of the buildings in red now exist, and those shown in yellow are to be built or renovated within the next 4 years. Below left, the Baraboo River bisects the museum's 60 acres. Below right, one of the daily summer demonstrations at the museum features the loading and unloading of circus wagons from flatcars, using real horsepower.

the visitor-lined parade route.

Legendary "Ringlingville"

Down the street from the Exhibit Hall are the many colorful barns and original brick structures of the Ringling Bros. Circus, which wintered in Baraboo from 1884 through 1918.

The Camel Barn, Ring Barn, Elephant Barn, Wild Animal House and the Ringling Office have all been designated "National Historic Landmarks" by the U.S. federal government and are highlights of the present-day Circus World Museum.

Within these buildings and throughout this hallowed site, visitors are reminded of the hustle and bustle of "Ringlingville", as the circus prepared for each new season in its winter quarters.

"Under a billowing, blue canvas big top, the time-honored traditions of the sawdust ring are presented by a host of gifted performers assembled from around the world. From the 2,000 seats circling the perimeter of the huge tent, audiences cheer the heroics of animal

trainers, aerialists, high-wire walkers, jugglers, hand-balancing acrobats, bareback riders, resident clowns and, of course, the elephants.

"A blaring brass band, production numbers, lavish sequined costumes, showgirls, theatrical lighting and a singing ringmaster lend their enhancement as the story of the circus is told. It

THROUGHOUT THE SUMMER, audiences are treated to two classic circus performances a day, "one of the best shows in North America".

THE ELEGANT Columbia Bandwagon (right) was the very first parade wagon in the Circus World Museum's collection, 1958. Funding from the Great Circus Parade enables the museum to collect and restore such priceless gems as the Bostock and Wombwell Bandchariot (opposite page). Built in 1856, it is the oldest parade wagon in existence. See Chapter 6 for more.

is truly a classic circus performance—one of the best in North America.

Historic Gems

The Circus World Museum possesses the world's largest collection of circus wagons—over 150 glittering masterpieces. The funding for wagon restoration is one of the enormous benefits received from the museum's annual staging of the Great Circus Parade.

Moreover, the Great Circus Parade has provided the financial support that enabled the Circus World Museum to acquire and restore such wood-carved treasures as the 137 year-old Bostock &

Wombwell Bandchariot, the oldest circus wagon in existence.

Throughout the Museum grounds,

"The Circus World Museum possesses the world's largest collection of circus wagons—over 150 glittering masterpieces..."

colossal circus wagons are found everywhere. About 40 are positioned in the

W.W. Deppe Wagon Pavilion, where dockets offer informative anecdotes about the history of each.

Several wagons may be found along the circus midway. Others grace many additional exhibit buildings. The menagerie tent houses several antique cage wagons, and the circus "backyard" is filled with generator wagons, seat wagons, office wagons and dressing room wagons.

Some of the sparkling gems in the museum's wagon collection merit special recognition. The Ringling Bros. Bell Wagon, with its cathedral chimes, is per-

THE ROBERT L. PARKINSON Library and Research Center is the world's only library devoted entirely to the circus.

THE LATE Robert Parkinson, pictured below with Wisconsin Governor Tommy Thompson, managed the library and served as its chief historian. He played a major role in staging the Great Circus Parade for 25 years.

THE LIBRARY'S COLLECTION is unparalleled and its value is literally priceless.

haps the most unique circus wagon in existence. Barnum & Bailey's Two-Hemispheres Bandwagon is the largest ever built. The Golden Age of Chivalry and the Cinderella Float are spine-tingling to behold.

So Much More

Each year more than 200,000 visitors journey to Circus World where they are treated to a fabulous fantasia of family fun. There are steam calliope concerts, an adorable giraffe to admire, cotton candy and fresh lemonade, an old-fashioned carousel, elephant rides, a miniature circus layout, rousing band organs and old circus railroad cars with walk-through exhibits.

"A fast-paced stage show called "The

"Each year more than 200,000 visitors journey to Circus World, where they are treated to a fabulous fantasia of family fun..."

Mysteries of Magic" relates the heritage of well-known illusionists who appeared at circuses at one time or another—Harry Houdini from Appleton, Wisconsin among them.

For visitors interested in seeing the site of the first Ringling Bros. performance, or the mansions built by the brothers after their rags-to-riches rise to circus fame, a trolley ride throughout the city is offered.

The Circus World Museum employees rely almost exclusively on the Robert L. Parkinson Library and Research Center. For the preparation and mounting of new exhibits, searching for new costume designs and for details required for accurate wagon restoration, the library is indispensable.

The library houses an amazing aggregation of posters, pictures, trade journals, books, tickets, programs, route information, artwork and original source material, to name but a few categories of memorabilia on file and carefully indexed.

The Library and Research Center is open as a public service facility on a year-round basis. Its staff assists with hundreds of research projects conducted by individuals, businesses and universities from all over the world. The library's collection is unparalleled and its value is literally priceless.

The Great Circus Parade is a vital outreach program which the museum and its staff are quite proud of. The Board of Directors of the Circus World Museum is grateful to the Great Circus Parade, Inc. for making the parade in Milwaukee possible and for supporting our efforts to enhance this wonderful museum.

As our dedicated staff looks boldly toward the future of this expanding institution, allow us to personally invite you to come visit us. Step back into the golden days of the American circus with a journey through the Circus World Museum soon.

Greg's exciting narrative hits the nail on the head. Over 5 million people have purchased tickets to the museum since it opened its doors for the first time, and nary a person has gone home disappointed. Everyone enjoys their visit.

YOUNG AND OLD ALIKE. The museum, with its exhibits, parades, animals, shady grounds (and refreshments!), has a pace to suit just about everybody.

FOR VISITORS interested in seeing the site of the first Ringling Bros. performance or the mansions built by the brothers after their rags-to-riches rise to fame, the museum offers a trolley ride through the city.

Ron Brayer

Greg Parkinson, the Executive Director of the Circus World Museum.

Ron Brayer

HEADS UP! The audience has their eyes glued to the top of the dome. A tightrope walker perhaps?

A Year-Round Chore

The enormity and the complexity of the Great Circus Parade is such that work starts on next year's event as soon as the last notes of the Steam Calliope fade off into the distance!

The Circus World Museum and the Great Circus Parade, Inc. are two separate groups with many of the same goals. Without the Great Circus Parade, Inc., the museum could never dream of staging the parade—it's too expensive.

And without the Circus World Museum, all the money in the world couldn't stage the parade. In short, neither organization can function without the other, and the great success of the parade is a result of the efficiency in which these two groups work together.

I could fill this whole book with the names of people that help put on the parade every year, and the work that each one of them does. But for the sake of brevity, here is a quick synopsis of some of the major responsibilities we have to tackle.

First, we study the videotapes of the parade. We take note of what looked sloppy, or appeared out of time. We examine every detail that could be improved upon, and vow to change it for the next year's parade.

Ben Barkin begins the year with the most important job of all: Raising the necessary funds to keep the show on the road. Ben relies on decades worth of contacts and dazzling publicity releases, created from the year's best photos, to help lure sponsorship.

Joe Weinfurter and Jack Varic pitch in to start the ball rolling again by writing thank-you notes, answering letters, cleaning up any loose ends and paying the final bills.

Directing the Parade

When I left Baraboo in 1972, Bob Parkinson took my place as Director of the parade. Then the Great Circus Parade was discontinued until 1985, at which time Bob Parkinson again took charge. He handled this parade chore through

42   THE CIRCUS WORLD MUSEUM

CIRCUS LOVERS of all ages pass through a traditional menagerie on their way to the big top. Paul Ingrassia (below left) is the current Director of the Great Circus Parade.

Ron Brayer

N OBSTINATE OSTRICH waits for visitors the menagerie tent.

Nancy Cutlip

THE MENAGERIE tent exhibits tigers, giraffes, camels and, of course, elephants.

1988. Then because his work load was so overwhelming, he relinquished the parade job to Dave Sa Loutos. Eventually, Bob was able to concentrate his efforts on managing the Circus World Museum's Library and Research Center, which was named for him after his death in 1990.

Dave Sa Loutos was Parade Director for 1989; then he, too, gave up the task to a longtime friend of the parade and museum, Paul Ingrassia, who had just recently retired from business.

Like everyone involved with the parade, Paul's lifetime hobby is the circus. He has therefore been acquainted with the Circus World Museum since its inception.

An important aspect of Paul's position involves contacting and lining up the hundreds of horsemen that are so essential to the parade effort. Their confirmation and willingness to participate must be secured very early in the year.

The same is true with clown units, marching bands, bands that will ride on top of the big wagons, special units and over a hundred volunteer circus buffs.

Paul must prepare himself for last-minute cancellations. If a clown drops out of the parade at the last minute, Paul can shrug it off. However, if he finds out that a man expected to supply an eight-horse team for a bandwagon has a serious sickness at home and won't be able to come to Milwaukee—Paul must act—and fast.

He has a list of team owners waiting in the wings for an assignment. He just hopes one man with the right kind of team will say "yes" at the last minute.

It is also the responsibility of the Circus Parade Director to work with the Director of the Circus World Museum, Greg Parkinson, to develop new parade features. For instance, new wardrobes are planned, designed and created.

Also, each year, Paul and Greg decide which of the massive parade wagons need to be ran through the workshop for an overhaul or a new coat of paint. This is done annually so all the parading wagons are in tip-top shape.

The Great Circus Train presents yet another huge undertaking. First, the route is determined and approved. Then federal inspectors are called in to check each and every railroad car. The Chicago and Northwestern Railroad Inspectors double-check everything. Since we use antique flatcars, and sometimes an old steam locomotive, safety is always the first priority.

Finally, we establish the parade route through the downtown Milwaukee streets. The Street Department is con-

> *"The mission of the Circus World Museum is to collect, preserve and present the history of the American circus in the form of an educational living-history museum."*

tacted in order to prevent a major repair project or sewer work from interfering with the parade route.

Joe Weinfurter, in the Milwaukee office, is in touch with the Police Department, Fire Department, City Hall, Milwaukee County Executive's Office, Red Cross Communications, the Transit System, the fireworks group, reviewing stands, emergency ambulance service, bleacher seats, toilet service, waste receptacles, chartered buses, and on and on.

Joe also handles the pre-parade details such as lining up the antique cars, high wheel men and their bikes and other special units. Additionally, Joe handles the annual brochure. He develops the layout, photographs and quotations as well as other printing jobs such as invitations, tickets and passes.

Each year both offices have their frustrations, but I don't hear too many complaints out of them. We all enjoy our work, and it shows. These men in charge have never let the public down. The Great Circus Parade continues to be bigger and better than ever.

THE MUSIC AND COLOR of the street parade is a daily ritual in the summertime.

Parade Wardrobe Is A Mammoth Challenge

I n the mid to late 1800s, when competition was fierce among the traveling circuses of the day, press agents had to have a real knack for words when it came to describing their street parade.

"Our Street Parade," one would say, "is a mighty catalog of wonders, crimsoned with the radiant luster of the morning sun."

Or another would proclaim that his circus parade was "the largest, richest, rarest and most generously resplendent display ever."

This onslaught of adjectives was largely an effort to convey one thing: The stunning visual effect the Wardrobe Department has on the parade. In the circus, men and women wear wardrobe. Horses, ponies, zebras, elephants and

AN EQUESTRIAN TROUPE outfitted in Turkish wardrobe adds an exciting flair to the procession.

camels wear trappings.

In preparing for the Great Circus Parade, the Circus World Museum staff meticulously studies old circus posters and hundreds of old photographs. Every garment is constructed in an attempt to authentically duplicate a historic circus street parade.

One single outfit for a girl and the horse she's riding might include:

- ➤ Jacket
- ➤ Gloves
- ➤ Skirt
- ➤ Saddle blanket
- ➤ Petticoat
- ➤ Chest covering
- ➤ Ascot
- ➤ Bridle Covering
- ➤ Hat with Plume
- ➤ Rein Covering
- ➤ Shoes

There are literally hundreds of costumed participants in the parade each year, so you can realize the quantity of items that must be designed, produced, identified, stored and distributed. And to top off the complexity of the job, each and every participant in the entire parade has an outfit tailor-made for him.

The Great Circus Parade would settle for nothing less. Neither do the hundreds of thousands of people watching the event—in fact, many of their cheers, whistles and ovations are applauding the parade's spine-tingling display of costumes.

Fitting Every Participant

A good portion of the Wardrobe Department's energy is spent making costumes for the six marching bands in the parade. Each band features 100 or more high school kids—and every one of them has to be fitted, which often seems to be a never-ending task.

The bands are all outfitted in historical themes. One band is dressed in clown outfits, another dressed patriotic style. One band is outfitted as Cossacks, and another as Queen Victoria's Guard. Additionally, there are six or eight smaller bands that play from on top of wagons, all in appropriate historical wardrobe as well.

There are 10 carriages in the parade,

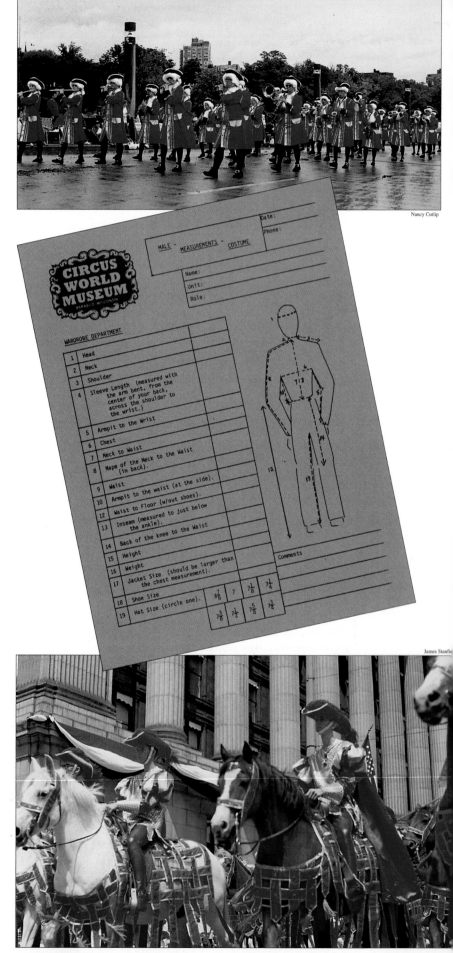

James Stanfie

COSTUMES are tailor-made to fit every member of the several 100-piece bands feature in the parade. Above, mounted buglers show off the Wardrobe Department's handiwork

THE PAWNEE BILL BANDWAGON appropriately features a band dressed as cowboys. Below, members of Queen Victoria's Guard Band are getting ready to march.

PEG COBURN'S eagle eye spots some necessary adjustments.

Joy Lewis

EXQUISITE DETAIL can be seen on costume worn by an equestrienne at left. Above, Mayme Ward was the first to head the Wardrobe Department, during the Schlitz years. The Baraboo High School Band (right) in colorful clown wardrobe is an annual attraction. At lower left is the beautiful Rainbow Equestrienne Troupe.

Jim Merrill

and several important personages ride in each vehicle. They are usually dressed in elaborate turn-of-the-century wardrobe. The carriage drivers and brakemen are similarly attired.

The Men in Red

The Wardrobe Department has simulated the garments that were worn by the drivers and brakemen in the circus parades of yesteryear. The red jackets, pants and pith helmets featured on the crew of the more than 70 historic circus wagons in the parade are replicated right down to the buckles.

The outriders and out-walkers (assistants to the wagons and animal processions) are outfitted in a similar fashion, except that they wear red caps instead of pith helmets.

All told, there are nearly 1,000 participants in each parade that have to pass through our Wardrobe Department. There are no exceptions to this rule. It might seem picky, but I feel that one uncostumed participant can throw off the entire effect.

Obviously, the Wardrobe Department represents an integral aspect of the

"Every participant in the entire parade has an outfit tailor-made for him..."

parade, and a fantastic chore. The person in charge has to design, create, organize and, above all, have the know-how to get the task done in authentic circus style.

The Great Circus Parade has such a person in Peg Coburn. I first met Peg in the mid '70s when I was working for Ringling Bros. and Barnum & Bailey in central Florida, where I had the opportunity to observe her magnificent work for many years.

When we decided to bring the Great Circus Parade back in 1985, I knew just

"All told, there are nearly 1,000 participants in each parade that have to pass through our Wardrobe Department..."

who to call. Peg came to Baraboo for an interview, and was immediately hired to head up the Wardrobe Department.

Peg had tremendous talent in this field, and had learned all the tricks of the trade from her many years of experience with Ringling Bros.

For example, an elephant robe, or blanket, as it is called, is not just a beautiful piece of material draped over the beast. It would not last for two blocks before it was all pulled apart. Elephants, like people come in different sizes, and have different shaped bodies. So each animal is fitted with his very own trapping.

The robe must be lined with a light weight canvas to absorb body sweat and withstand the abrasive wear caused by the rough hide. Steel rings are sewed into the right places to attach girth straps. Buckles hold the robe, for the animal's roly-poly body quakes with each step. Finally, each robe is marked with the elephant's name.

A similarly demanding process is repeated for every camel, horse and pony in the parade.

Updating History

Meetings take place to plan the parade for the following year several months before the parade. Changing the wardrobe is one way we keep the parade looking fresh to the people who watch it every year, including ourselves.

Peg always has lots of suggestions for changes or improvements in the historic costumes. We all decide which are the most flashy, unique and appealing, then Peg draws color sketches of what she has just described to us.

Once the sketch is approved, Peg orders all of the necessary material,

NEW COSTUMES are designed and created for the parade every year. When Peg Coburn's sketches are approved, she orders all of the material and begins sewing. Below, authentic baggage wagons conveniently store wardrobe at the Circus World Museum.

THE CAMEL TROUPE is trained and owned by Dave Hale. The Great Circus Parade pays tribute to many different cultures.

sequins, jewels, tape or cord, crystals, velvets, satins, crepes, corduroy, cockades or ostrich plumes required. Her personal files contain the names and addresses of the sources for all of the material and accoutrements.

This material is very special. It must be strong and durable—able to hold up in the rain—yet retain an elegant appearance. Peg knows exactly how to accommodate both.

A Smooth Setup

As the apparel for each new unit is finished, it is put on hangers, covered with plastic bags and hung in one of the wardrobe wagons. There are eight of these cavernous baggage wagons. Some are fitted with racks to hold the wardrobe hangers. Others are equipped with shelves for hats, or cabinets for small items.

All of the wagons, of course, are watertight. Each has a set of portable

THE STAFF at the Circus World Museum studies old circus posters to authentically reproduce the wardrobe. For example, compare the photos at right and above with the poster on the facing page.

steps stored underneath it, in racks. A list of the contents of each wagon corresponds to a number painted on the side.

At the Circus World Museum, the Wardrobe Department is located in a building of its own. Peg's workshop is located in a large corner area. The wardrobe wagons are all lined up in the rear

of the building, with their steps in place—a most convenient setup.

After each parade, Peg's department must immediately dry out each piece. If it isn't wet from the rain, it might be from perspiration. Each piece is checked to be sure a button is not missing, or a skirt is not torn. Then the

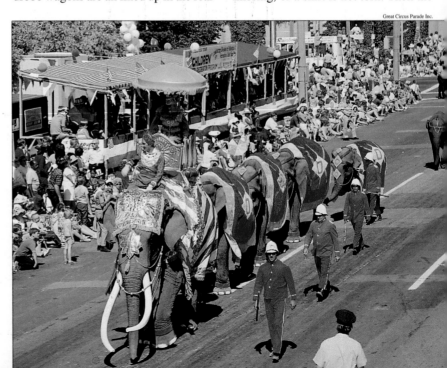

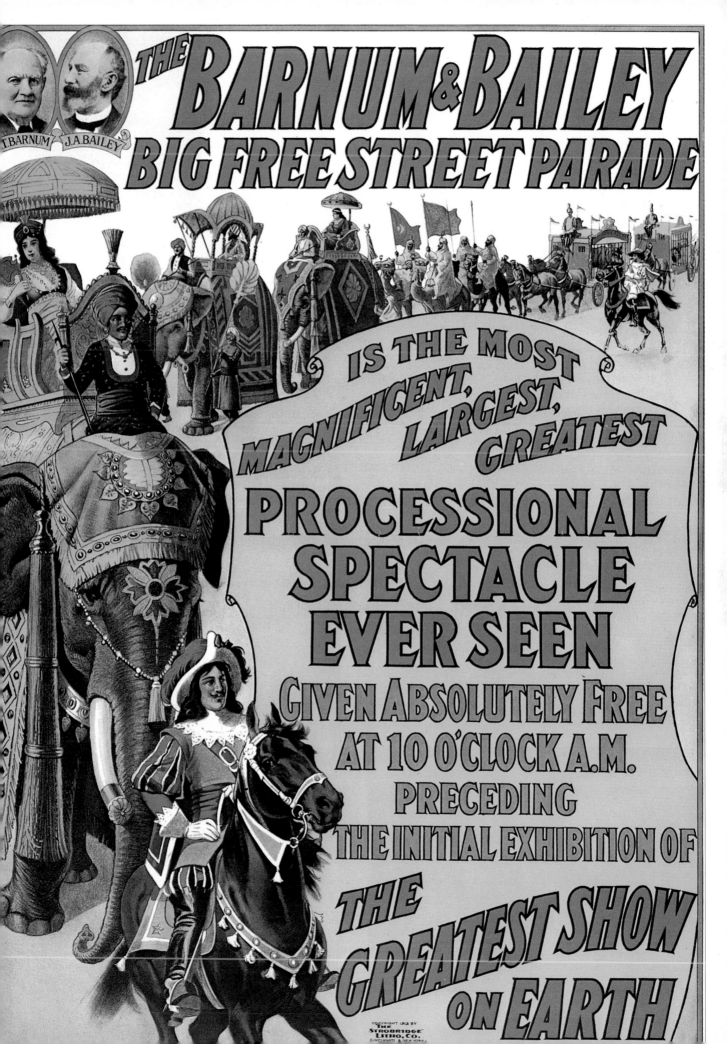

dry cleaners get into the act.

One final check is done before the whole outfit is put away for the winter. For example, if there are 18 girls in the equestrienne troupe, there must be 36 gloves. Do all the hats have plumes? Is

"Peg has tremendous talent in this field...she learned all the tricks of the trade from her many years of experience with Ringling Bros."

anything broken? If so, everything is repaired or replaced so there are no surprises the next year.

The Great Circus Parade Wardrobe Department represents an enormously complex operation that somehow runs like clockwork.

All of the diligence pays off when the procession rolls down the streets of Milwaukee.

It is a veritable kaleidoscope of color and flash. Or, as one circus press agent described his street parade 100 years ago, "The avenues are ablaze with prismatic hues of circus colors— eyes are dazzled and heads set a whirling."

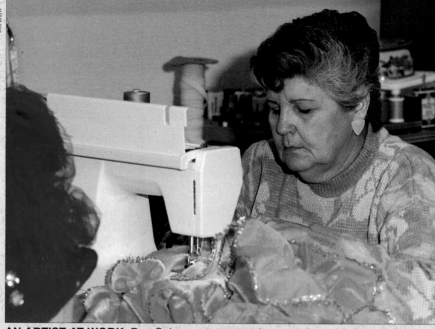

AN ARTIST AT WORK, Peg Coburn creates another stunning period costume.

LYNN BIALK as Annie Oakley at left. Below, each draft horse wears a feather plume on the bridle. Riders at lower left are outfitted in lavish medieval costumes.

EDITH BARNHART sat astride her very well-trained horse in a presentation of the Sells-Floto Circus parade of the 1920s.

AMERICAN QUARTER HORSE ASSOCIATION provides the parade with a troupe of rugged riders.

A PROUD AMERICAN INDIAN CHIEF in full headdress is an inspiring sight in the Great Circus Parade in the early 1960s.

COWBOYS RIDE THE RANGE, only this time atop the Gollmar Bros. Tableau. The colorful Wild West section of the parade celebrates the history of the American Frontier.

Lots of Excitement Aboard
The Great Circus Train

O h, what a glorious sight it is for us aboard the Great Circus Train. We see families sitting on lawn chairs in fields, crowds gathered at country crossroads, people lounging in their backyards…waving, whistling, calling out as the half-mile, 31-car procession-

al chuggs on by. It is wonderful.

"There were miles and miles of smiles," said Ernie Borgnine after his first time aboard the Circus Train.

The 2-day journey from Baraboo to downtown Milwaukee passes through dozens of towns as it spans the Wisconsin and Illinois countryside at a

leisurely pace. Over bridges, through green valleys and across open fields, the low bellowing horn of the Great Circus Train signals its coming.

News releases have been sent to newspapers in every town and village along the route explaining our arrival. The spectacle is so colorful and over-

Joanne Peterson

A FEW MILES south of Janesville, Wisconsin, the Great Circus Train crosses a beautiful old stone bridge at the town of Tiffany.

whelming that thousands plan their day around the scheduled appearance of the train! Many rural and city people that can't make it to Milwaukee for the street parade on Sunday are treated to a weekday event that is every bit as dazzling.

While en route, the Circus Train is limited to a maximum speed of 30 mph. This slow speed seems to suit everybody just fine. The tens of thousands of people waiting to see the colorful train are able to feast their eyes and savor the unusual sight for a longer span of time.

Just Like the Old Days

Circuses began relying on the railroads in the 1870s, and for many years the two went hand in hand. Reuniting the partnership has added a whole new dimension to the event

In 1965, the Circus World Museum crew was thrilled to add the Circus Train to Parade Week. As a historic institution, it is our job to reenact circus history. Every element we add to that scenario takes people back in time a little further.

Like the parade, the entire Circus Train operation is carried out in its historical context. Dapple gray Percherons

---

"Dapple gray Percherons load and unload the parade wagons onto flatcars—just as the big circuses did years ago…"

---

load and unload the parade wagons on to flatcars—just as the big circuses did years ago. Chock blocks hold the wagons in place. Even the railroad cars are restored originals from some of the big circuses of yesterday like Ringling Bros. and Barnum & Bailey.

On some years, the Circus Train uses steam locomotives—and these relics are truly a wonderful sight. But the added cost to rent them was enormous, and their reliability dubious, so Chicago and Northwestern furnishes sparkling newly painted diesel locomotives.

As an example, the consist of the 1972 Circus Train was as follows: There were two stock cars. One was used to carry the horses necessary for loading and unloading the train. The other stock car was used to carry miscellaneous cir-

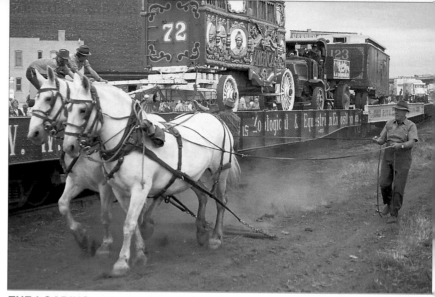

THE LOADING and unloading of circus wagons onto the flatcars has become a crowd favorite during parade week.

JOHN HERRIOTT (center) watches carefully: One blast from the whistle will stop the team…two blasts means go ahead.

TEAMS OF PERCHERONS and replicated runs, jacks and pulleys employ the same operation pioneered by the Ringling Bros. Circus in the mid-1800s. The process is quite toilsome for the more than 70 wagons, but it adds to the authenticity of the reenactment.

cus paraphernalia.

Then came 22 flatcars that were loaded with 89 wagons and vehicles.

Last on the train were the Santa Fe Diner, two Pullmans and two open-air cars. These last five cars carried about 200 people, including sponsors and their representatives, local and state officials and, of course, employees of the Circus World Museum.

Luck Played a Part

About a half-mile up the Baraboo River from the Circus World Museum lies the original Ringling Bros. Circus Railroad Car Shops. Built in the late 19th century, this 13-acre piece of property strategically adjoined the Chicago and Northwestern Railroad tracks.

The main building was 600 feet long and had three railroad tracks running the full length. In addition, there were hundreds of feet of track on the property for storing railroad cars.

When the Ringling Bros. Circus left its Baraboo headquarters in 1918, this unusual piece of property was bought by the North American Refrigerator Car Corporation. They used it for repairing their railroad cars.

In 1964, I found out that this property was for sale, and had been for the last couple of years. Their railroad car repairing service had been moved to another city where the facilities were more up to date.

Historically, I knew this piece of property should belong to the Circus World Museum. So, in early 1964, I approached the company, thinking that if they could not sell the property, they might benefit by giving it to the Circus World Museum. And this they did. I guess they thought this was a godsend solution to their problem. So did I.

In the chain of events toward acquiring the Great Circus Train, the above was a very important step, but I did not realize it at the time.

Saw the Opportunity

In 1963 and 1964, the first 2 years we paraded in Milwaukee, all of the wagons were hauled into the city on lowboys and flatbed trucks. To say the least, this was a very clumsy way to do the job.

Then I read an ad in *Amusement Business* magazine that stated all the equipment of the World of Mirth Carnival would be auctioned in September 1964, including their railroad cars. I really perked up.

These 70-foot-long flatcars were

THOUSANDS OF WISCONSIN AND ILLINOIS RESIDENTS turn out along the route to see the Circus Train pass by. They smile and wave at the passengers, and the passengers wave back.

THE COLORFUL TRAIN looks almost like a toy as it chugs through the lush Wisconsin countryside. Below, the Circus Train crosses the Wisconsin River near Merrimac.

specifically built for circuses. This could be a golden opportunity to improve the Great Circus Parade!

Quickly, I gathered a fine selection of photographs of circus trains of 50 and 60 years ago, showing them en route and unloading with huge crowds watching the action.

The next step was to present the idea to Ben Barkin. As usual, he instantly

"Ben Barkin quickly realized the potential."

realized the additional exposure his client, Schlitz, and the Circus World Museum would receive.

We discussed the estimated budget and other related problems. Then we went to see Bob Uihlein—to get his blessing. I went through the entire presentation, after which he agreed to the idea of a circus train.

"But," he said, "I have a question for you. Where are you going to store the railroad cars when they're not in use?"

"Well," I said, "we just happen to have a 600-foot-long building with three sets of tracks that run the full length." I explained our recent 13-acre gift from the North American Refrigerator Car Corporation.

Sealing the Deal

Accompanied by the general foreman and the trainmaster of the Southern Railroad, I visited the Winston Salem yards to see what the World of Mirth Carnival had to offer. Mr. R.W. Apple was in control of all the carnival equipment.

We sorted through the cars and found some historic beauties: cars that had been built specially for hauling circus wagons. We purchased 12 flatcars and one stock car, and the Great Circus Train was born!

The Southern Railroad took the cars into its shop to check them over and make sure all air brake systems functioned properly. On October 16 the Southern wired that the cars were en route. They arrived in Baraboo on October 30, 1964.

Later, Mr. Apple called and said he had five more flatcars that he had to get rid of. I explained that we had all we could use at the moment, but could possibly use more next year if we enlarged the Circus Train.

Mr. Apple said he could not pay

SCORES OF PEOPLE waiting at each of the stations whistle, cheer and applaud the joyous arrival of the Great Circus Train. Below, a crowd is treated to a steam calliope concert.

Joanne Peterson

THE TRAIN makes several brief stops and one overnight stay during its 2-day journey to Milwaukee. In all, people in about 40 towns are able to witness the half-mile-long spectacle.

Jim Morrill

demurage for a year. I told him we had hundreds of feet of empty track here in Baraboo on which there would be no demurrage, if he would ship them to Baraboo. He did this, and as it turned out, we did enlarge the train and were able to purchase these five flatcars the next year at a real knockdown price.

Research showed us that these cars had been used by such names as Hagenbeck-Wallace Circus, Sparks Circus, Tim McCoy's Wild West and Ringling Bros. and Barnum & Bailey. They were a tremendous historical acquisition for the Circus World Museum as well as a practical means of transporting and displaying the wagon collection.

Refurbishing Was a Big Job

Now came the job of refurbishing these railroad cars. The first thing we did was rip off the old wood decking. Then we sandblasted the cars and put on a coat of primer followed by a coat of paint. The crew then installed new plank decking on all the flatcars.

The big job was to letter the sides of these cars with various circus names. We decided that each car would carry the title of a big railroad circus of years ago. Cal Bergner, and his wife, Maida, were assigned this task. As a team, the Bergners did all of the lettering on wagons, signs or museum buildings.

Lettering the cars was a tough assignment because we were only able to bring the temperature up to 50° in the old building—and it was the dead of winter.

So Cal built a framed hut with plastic sides and furnished it with electric heaters. The side against the railroad car was open so they could paint. It was a rugged and miserable assignment, but this talented team got the job done.

All the cars on the Circus Train are beautiful, and millions of people who have enjoyed watching the train wind through the countryside will agree.

Added Passenger Cars

Eventually we needed additional cars to carry people. Schlitz authorized me to talk to the Pullman Co. that had dozens of beautiful cars for sale at $5,000 each. After parading through many of these cars, I picked two combination cars; those that had seating areas as well as compartments or berths.

I explained that the museum was as poor as church mice and that the cars would be used only once a year for our Circus Train. The Pullman management softened and gave us two cars for $5,000.

FOR THE PASSENGERS of the Circus Train, there is an abundance of food, drink and fun. The Razmatazz performs turn-of-the-century music appropriate to the period of circus parades.

WISCONSIN GOVERNOR Tommy Thompson (right) is eager to climb aboard the train in Baraboo and enjoy the excitement.

MILWAUKEE POLICE Captain Jeffrey Bialk (left) and his wife, Lynn, rode on the Circus Train. Lynn rides as Annie Oakley in the Wild West section of the parade.

Jim Morrill

THE CIRCUS TRAIN on the lakefront, approaching Milwaukee. Below, the Chicago and Northwestern train depot looms up ahead.

Frankie B. Cole

Jim Morrill

I then contacted Fred Gurley, Chairman of the Board of the Santa Fe. My question to him was, "Did they have any old dining cars laying around that

> *"The Chicago and Northwestern played a big part in assisting the Circus Train in its beginnings..."*

they were about to scrap? We could sure use one on our Circus Train." He said that he'd check around for me.

About 3 weeks later I had a phone call from the freight agent in Baraboo. "I want to see you," he said. When I came into his office he said, "Sit down." He was furiously "chain chewing" his

spearmint gum.

"I have a Santa Fe diner out here that we hauled from Chicago for nothing. Last year we hauled those two cars of Disney Wagons for nothing," he said. "The Northwestern is going broke hauling your freight."

He showed me the diner. It was an absolute beauty and fully equipped. As it turned out, Fred Gurley had pulled this car out of mothballs in Kansas City and shipped it to the Circus World Museum as a present.

As for the Chicago and Northwestern freight agent? Come Christmas I gave him three cartons of Wrigley's

Spearmint, which I figured must be a year's supply.

Later we added two open-air cars to

SIX DAYS later, after 2 days with the train, 3 days at the show grounds and finally the parade, the whole process is repeated. Everything is packed up and loaded back onto the train for the trip home to Baraboo.

Frankie B. Cale

the train. These were old railway express baggage cars that were given to the museum by the Milwaukee Railroad. It took some engineering to redesign these cars for use on the Circus Train, but they have been completely safe and extremely popular with our passengers.

With the necessary cars in our "back pocket" so to speak, the next step was to develop the equipment necessary to load and unload the wagons from the flatcars.

Fortunately, I had observed this operation closely, even photographed it through the 1930's and 1940's with the big railroad circuses.

Horses Load Wagons

We had to build runs (ramps on which the wagon could roll); jacks to support the runs; cross-overplates between cars; chocks to hold wagons in place; snubbing posts for braking a descending wagon; pull-up and pull-over ropes for the horses; and possum bellies, the compartments slung under the flatcars that carried other necessary equipment.

The first couple of years, Gene Traxler and his crew handled the loading and unloading of the train. Gene operated in Baraboo and had a well-coordinated crew. He handled the specialized job with great efficiency.

Later, John Herriott, the Circus Performance Director at the Circus World Museum, took over. John had been in the circus business all his life and had lots of know-how. Together we mustered a fine group of circus buffs who came in from all over the United States to volunteer their services. The Circus Train presented a lot of work, but it has always managed to pay off.

Help from Railroads

While all the railroad cars and their loads of wagons belonged to the Circus World Museum, we contracted with the Chicago and Northwestern Railway to haul them from Baraboo to Milwaukee and back, over their tracks.

They, of course, furnished the locomotives and the train crew. So we were in the hands of experts who went all out to handle our train with great dispatch and care.

Year after year, the Circus Train continues to attract throngs of people. For nostalgia, fun and authenticity, it adds a whole new dimension to the week-long event known as the Great Circus Parade.

THE CIRCUS TRAIN hugs the rocky banks of Devil's Lake near Baraboo.

TRAINMASTER John Herriott and Chappie, (right) happy with the success but exhausted, grab forty winks on the way back to Baraboo in 1967.

FOR MANY YEARS, the railroad and the circus went hand in hand. Reuniting the partnership in 1965 has added a whole new dimension to the parade.

Collecting and Restoring Parade Wagons Rescued A Piece of the Past

Since the very first parade, in 1963, I have always taken a special delight in stirring the curiosities of the public. Every year while I'm at the parade or hanging around the show grounds, people approach me. I must be pretty easy to spot.

From children to reporters to old-timers, folks wonder about every different aspect of the parade you could ever imagine. I find myself bombarded with questions, which I love to answer...but I can barely watch the action!

Most of the questions people have pertain to the wagon collection.

Where did you get that wagon? *How* old is it? If it's a hundred years old, *why* does it look so good? *Who* refinishes them? *What* are they worth? And on and on and on.

This chapter is written with those questions in mind...for anyone who wants to take a closer look into the heart and soul of the Great Circus Parade.

The collection of about 150 antique parade wagons in the Circus World Museum is valued at over 5 million dol-

C.P. Fox Collection

The Barnum & Bailey Greatest Show on Earth

SECTION 1 - SHOWING THE GREAT 40 HORSE TEAM AND PONDEROUS TABLEAU BAND WAGON OF THE TWO HEMISPHERES. THIS ONE VEHICLE AND TEAM REPRESENTING AN OUTLAY OF OVER $50,000.

THE WORLD'S LARGEST, GRANDEST, BEST, AMUSEMENT INSTITUTION.

lars. But to me they are literally priceless. Why?

Well for one, they represent an era; a page of history that you can reach out and touch. So much from the past has been lost or forgotten...I sometimes think of these circus wagons as an endangered species...saved from extinction in the nick of time.

Then there is the art! Folk art, I call it, because each wagon was designed and built to represent a different theme.

Peter S. Draves

IN 1903 the Barnum & Bailey Circus unveiled the magnificent 8-ton Two Hemispheres Bandwagon. Powered by a massive 40-horse hitch, this spectacle enthralled audiences throughout America before hitting the streets of Milwaukee in 1904. Below, the restored wagon repeating history some 85 years later on the Milwaukee lakefront.

Be it the Wild West, a nursery rhyme or the discovery of America, the wagon collection tells the story of our culture.

At one time wagon-making was a very esteemed craft—the woodcarving, sculpting and painting are simply remarkable. These wagons are extravagant, grand creations—from a time when most folks were leading simple, meager lives. That contrast has always touched me.

There are only a handful of people alive that still possess the knowledge and skill to reconstruct a circus wagon to its original glory. The men in the refurbishing shop at the Circus World Museum are the last of a dying breed…literally. In this chapter you will see these men in action as they transform rotting boards into glorious horse-drawn vehicles.

You will discover, in this chapter, that each wagon has two histories: one from the turn of the century, and one from the 1950s and '60s. The first history deals with the inception, design and use of each wagon for a particular circus, usually during the late 1800s and early 1900s. How these wagons managed to survive the decades is also interesting.

The second history begins in 1960, when I took over the directorship of

> ## "In all, the wagon collection adds up to quite a story…150 different stories actually, that span almost that many years."

the Circus World Museum. It is a little more personal, I must admit. You see, the Circus World Museum now possesses nearly every antique parade wagon in existence. Acquiring them took some work.

Tracing each surviving relic back to its origin was one matter—getting the owners to part with them was yet another. In some instances, up to 10 years of "negotiating" were required before I was able to acquire a wagon for the museum.

Acquiring each wagon represented a whole new set of circumstances, characters and often humorous situations.

It's hard for me to look at a single wagon without the memories flooding in. Most of them revolve around the kind and generous people that went out of their way to help the struggling museum.

Bringing the wagons home to Baraboo for a full restoration job—knowing thousands would be able to enjoy them was another wonderful feeling.

In all, the wagon collection adds up to quite a story…150 different stories, actually, that span almost that many years. It wasn't always easy getting my hands on them, but it sure was worth it.

And one more thing: This wagon collection belongs to all of us. Officially, they are the property of the tax-paying public. So come check them out on parade day this year. But please, read this chapter first! Because if you bump into me, I hope to be watching our wagons and the parade…not answering questions.

Sparking the Collection: The Very First Wagons

I HAD a couple of small signs in my office (the Ringling Red Ticket Wagon #123) that said, "You can't plow a field by turning it over in your mind—do it now". The other one said, "Diligence is the Mother of good luck".

Deciding that both were good advice, I set out to try to obtain as many beautiful, historic circus wagons as possible.

I was new on the job of running the Circus World Museum, which had been open to the public only a few months. I felt we had to have these big circus artifacts to make our museum special. What's more, in our possession they would be safe, restored and on display for thousands to enjoy.

Through previous research on my book *Circus Parades*, I knew where a good many wagons were located and was hoping they could find their way to Baraboo. I made phone calls and wrote letters by the hundreds. Contacts and word of mouth proved helpful, too.

The problem was, the wagons were scattered all over the United States: From Ft. Worth and Houston to Peoria and St. Louis. There were some in Cal-

THE COLUMBIA Bandwagon was built for the Barnum & Bailey Circus in 1902 and was the first wagon to arrive at the Circus World Museum, 57 years later.

ifornia, Nebraska, Indiana and even a nice collection in Northampton, England.

Remember this was '59—the first parade wasn't until '63. The museum at this point was little more than a couple of old Ringling Bros. barns, and likewise, as poor as a church mouse. I wasn't thinking about staging the parade yet, I just wanted to get the wagon collection under way.

Eventually, Schlitz got involved, people started recognizing the Circus World Museum and things got a lot easier. But for those first 4 years, it was "hammer and tongs" getting the initial 35 wagons that would later comprise the Great Circus Parade.

Let the Wagons Roll

The first wagon was acquired, appropriately enough, by Mr. John Kelley, the founder of the museum. He purchased the magnificent Columbia Bandwagon (built in 1900) from the defunct Cole Bros. Circus in 1957. It was in pretty decent shape when he brought it back from Bunker Hill, Indiana, but now it is spectacular—a real standout in the parade every year.

The second wagon we acquired was the Gollmar Bros. Mirror wagon from Peoria, Illinois. It's a beautiful bandwagon that was built in Baraboo around the turn of the century. I just had to bring this one home.

Trouble was, it was the property of the Peoria Zoo, and they had no intention of giving it up. So I talked to my friends at Pabst Brewery and was able to negotiate a trade. The Brewery bought three African lions and traded them to the zoo for the wagon, which they donated to the museum!

On a nearby Wisconsin farm once owned by Alf T. Ringling, a Roman racing chariot from the circus was found rotting away in a ravine. The farm owner, Howard Potter, presented this interesting vehicle to the Museum in 1960.

A small, but fascinating bandwagon from a California circus known as Norris & Rowe was found in a horse-drawn vehicle collection in San Francisco. The Norris & Rowe was a small circus that operated from 1900 to 1910. The wagon owner, Pierce A. Miller, agreed to sell it to the Circus World Museum for $150.00.

With no money at all to speak of, we were left with the problem of transporting the wagon to Baraboo. Then I

THE GOLLMAR BROS. Mirror Wagon was the second wagon in the museum's collection that now totals over 150. This wagon is also featured on the cover of this book.

remembered the Kenosha Auto Transport Co., a company that hauled cars all over the U.S. It struck me that these big trailers might come back from California empty.

Sure enough, a couple of friends in Milwaukee paved the way for me to meet Nick Demos, the president of Kenosha Auto Transport Co. On April 14, 1961, this wonderful circus wagon arrived in Baraboo, hauled free of charge.

A Modest Wagon

The next arrival was a tableau from the F.J. Taylor Circus. Historically, it was a rare find because no one knew it

SMALL BUT FASCINATING bandwagon built in 1900 was discovered in a horse-drawn vehicle collection in San Francisco.

existed. Through the efforts of circus historian Tom Parkinson and Floyd Henton, director of the Omaha, Nebraska Zoo, the beautiful wagon was found in a barn in a ravine just outside of Omaha.

It had been there so long, that trees 3 inches in diameter had grown all around it. We had to go back and get a chain saw to get it out of there!

Mrs. E.J. Larson, daughter of circus owner F.J. Taylor, presented the wagon to the museum in 1962. The whole Taylor family was just tickled that someone someone still cared about their old family circus and that their father would be remembered.

The F.J. Taylor was a small, relatively poor circus. Not all of our wagons came from the big guys like the Ringlings or Barnum. This was just a plain box body with a piece of painted canvas stretched across it. Some odds and ends woodcarvings had been attached to the corners. It certainly isn't one of the museum's most valu-able relics, but the humble care and attention that F.J. Taylor put into it make it one of my favorites.

A Rotting Shambles

In 1963 Schlitz purchased a hippo den from the Cole Bros. Circus that had been built in the '20s. It was a rotted shambles, but we had it shipped from Rochester, Indiana to Baraboo, where it was completely restored in the workshops of the museum.

In 1964 the Joseph Schlitz Brewing Co. began acquiring and presenting to the museum several interesting wag-

COVERED WAGON from the 101 Ranch Wild West show dates back to the 1860s.

ons from the Sparks Circus, Gollmar Bros. Circus and Howe's Great London Circus. They also presented us with a clown cart from Lemen Bros. Circus, a pony-sized Roman racing chariot from the Barnum & Bailey Circus, and four pony-sized wagons from the Terrell Jacobs Circus.

In 1965 the remains of the Robbins Bros. Air Calliope arrived in Baraboo. Again, a gift from Schlitz. This Air Calliope, still used in the Great Circus Parade, nearly met its end as a coal bin! Luckily we found it in Indiana, shoveled the coal out and brought it to the museum for restoration.

Finally, parade vehicles from the old wild west shows were not overlooked in establishing the collection. Wild west shows featured original covered wagons and stage coaches from the 1860s. Zack Miller Jr. of Ponca City, Oklahoma, whose father was one of the owners of

the 101 Ranch Wild West, presented two covered wagons from the old show, and Tony Diano of Canton, Ohio sold us a beautiful 1865 Concord stagecoach.

The Wagon Pavilion

Wagons were coming into the Circus World Museum by the mid-'60s so fast that we had no place to store them. This was a serious problem. We had to use empty sheds and barns all over town to keep them out of the winter snows!

I was in real trouble until I related the problems to Deane Adams, a restaurant owner in Madison, and Bob Pierce, Chairman of Wisconsin's Republican party.

These two guys were died-in-the-wool circus buffs and felt that the Circus World Museum was a super operation. Their enthusiasm was contagious, and before I knew it, they had contacted the State Building Commission.

They appropriated $150,000 to construct a 400-foot-long by 70-foot-wide pavilion in which to house and exhibit our beautiful wagons.

So we crossed another hurdle—let the wagons continue to roll into Baraboo.

It took every ounce of energy I had, but persistence, patience and persuasion did the job. The end result is the world's only grand collection of antique circus wagons and, of course, the inception of the Great Circus Parade.

The following sections include a photo-essay on wagon restoration followed by several more detailed narratives, more or less in chronological order, about how we acquired our major collections of wagons.

RATHER MODEST WAGON was a gift from descendants of the F.J. Taylor Circus.

A Walk Through the Wagon Restoration Shop

WHEN THE WAGONS began rolling into Baraboo in 1961, we found them in an array of conditions. There were those that could be classified as basket cases, like the barely recognizable Hippo Den. There were those in terrible shape—like the English Wagons—that were decaying rapidly, but still intact.

And some wagons were in pretty good shape, like the Bill Hames Collection. They had been neglected, but for the most part, protected from the elements. And some wagons, like the Disney Collection, despite being many decades old, arrived at the museum in extremely good condition.

In every case, it was the museum's first priority to retain as much of the wagons' original parts as possible. As a historical institution, we pride ourselves in restoring instead of replacing, though it many cases it would have been easier to just build a "replica".

Getting these wagons back into shape obviously presented a tremendous task. Ernie Zimmerly headed the crew to tackle these restoration jobs, and the Great Circus Parade, Inc. financed the work. Ernie was from the old school of work, work, work, and he loved the new challenges brought into the shop with each new wagon.

Then we found ourselves in desperate need of a blacksmith to assist Ernie. There just are not too many men left that possess these talents, so we were fortunate to locate Ron Dyer, a circus buff who was also an accomplished blacksmith.

Ron Dyer revived a forgotten art form when he produced circus pieces like goosenecks for wagon poles, hand holds, special hooks for safety chains and other equipment used for loading and unloading wagons from the train.

Eventually Ernie retired, and Marv Gauger jumped into the harness like an old fire horse, and began his masterful career of restoring circus wagons.

On a volunteer basis, Marv restored the Ringling Bell Wagon (an 1,100-hour task); Al G. Barnes' Circus Elephant Tableau; the Buffalo Bill Wild West Ticket Wagon; and the Ringling Pigmy Hippo Den.

In 1987, the decision was made to build an exact replica of the wagon The Ringling Bros. Circus used to haul their giraffe in 80 years ago. Marv worked from plans created from old photographs, and built a stunning vehicle in which to carry "Tu-Tall", our giraffe.

Gene Baxter

HIPPO DEN in its hey-day, around 1930 (above). Notice the "bay windows" that allow the hippo to turn around. Below, old photographs were invaluable in the restoring process. The next page chronicles the process of restoring this vehicle.

Author's Photo

THE HIPPO DEN was found in a field in Rochester, Indian (below left). Upon arriving in Baraboo for restoration (below each piece was marked, recorded and then put back togethe like a giant jigsaw puzzle. In the background is the 200-gallo water tank. Above, the finished product parading in Milwauke

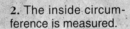

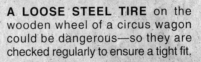

A LOOSE STEEL TIRE on the wooden wheel of a circus wagon could be dangerous—so they are checked regularly to ensure a tight fit.

1. The steel tire is first cut, removed from the wheel and cleaned up.

2. The inside circumference is measured.

3-4. Laying the tire in the hot coals causes the metal to expand.

5-6. Smoke from the burning wood adds to the uncomfortableness of the job as sledgehammers force the tire down onto the wheel.

7. Immersed in a tank of water and spun, the steel shrinks and then clamps snugly to the wheel.

(Photos from Author's Collection unless otherwise indicated.)

Joy Lewis

WOOD-CARVER Homer Daehn (above left) works diligently on the United States Bandwagon. Much of the original carving had to be restored, and some replaced. Below, the finished product appeared in the 1992 Great Circus Parade.

WAGON MASTER Marv Gauger (below left) headed the wagon shop until his retirement in 1987. The Elephant Tableau was built for the A. G. Barnes circus in the 1920s and required a great deal of restoration and wood carving when the museum received it in 1965.

B. G. Corbin

THE HISTORIC BUFFALO BILL Wild West Ticket Wagon was found in an apple orchard near Rochester, Indiana in 1968. It had come to an ignominious end as a chicken coop!

THIS IS THE
TICKET WAGON
FROM
BUFFALO BILL'S
WILD WEST SHOW
TO BE RESTORED THIS FALL

THE RESTORATION SHOP, on two occasions, has "replicated" wagons after an original, that is, built them from scratch. The unique vehicle below allowed "Tu-Tall", the Circus World Museum's resident giraffe, to join in the parade fun.

Ringling
BROS.

World's
Greatest
Shows

THE TOWERING
SKY REACHING
GIRAFFE

BUFFALO BILL'S
WILD WEST

TICKET
OFFICE

Ron Brayer

FULLY RESTORED and free of chickens, the Ticket Wagon, built in the 1890s, is said to be the only surviving vehicle from Buffalo Bill's legendary show.

THE 'AMERICA' STEAM CALLIOPE

THE AMERICA was built for the Cole Bros. circus in the early 1900s. The wood carvings on the sides depict the 12 peoples native to North, Central and South America. In 1940 the America was fitted with grillwork, a steam boiler and the calliope keyboard, and thus began a new and noisy career.

A DISASTROUS FIRE in February 1940 destroyed the main building of the Cole Bros. Circus in Rochester, Indiana. Many of their beautiful street parade wagons were lost, including their steam calliope.

A huge tableau wagon called The "America" survived the fire, as it had been stored elsewhere. When the Cole Bros. rebuilt their lost circus equipment, the America was called into service as a steam calliope.

Alterations were necessary, such as opening the roof and inserting grill-work on the upper sides so that steam could escape. A calliope the circus

obtained from an Ohio River boat and a boiler were installed. The America began a new and noisy life.

Then, in 1950, the Cole Bros. Circus folded. Its equipment was put into storage in an unused airplane hangar at the Bunker Hill Air Force Depot in Indiana. All of this information was common knowledge to me, as the circus was a serious hobby of mine.

Two years later I was reading *The Milwaukee Journal's* Green Sheet. The lead story was about Fred Hainer, the Vice President of Cleaver-Brooks. His company manufactured boiler equipment, and he thought having a steam

calliope would be a super way to promote his company at conventions and state fairs.

The story went on to say his diligent search had drawn a blank. He claimed there simply wasn't a steam calliope to be had in the U.S. As a result, he had reluctantly settled on an air calliope.

So I called Mr. Hainer and told him that I knew where he could possibly get a honest-to-goodness historic steam calliope.

After a long pause, he said, "Mr. Fox, you are dead wrong. I have searched this country over and there just are not any steam calliopes."

"Mr. Hainer," I said, "I am compiling a pictorial history of the circus street parades of years ago. It's being printed right now. I tell you, there is a steam calliope that might be available." I relayed the history of the Cole Bros. fire and the transformation of the America.

"Let me do a little checking," he responded, "and I'll get back to you."

Two days later, he called and said, "If you are not doing anything on Saturday, do you want to fly down to the Bunker Hill Air Force Depot with me?" "You bet your boots I do," was my quick answer. On the way down, Fred told me he was authorized to spend $2,500, but he hoped to get the America for less from the defunct circus.

Arrangements had been made to let us into this enormous airplane hangar, so in we went. What we saw was, for me, a sad sight. All of the wagons that had at one time been so beautiful were run-down and decaying in the dark.

Then I spotted the America, and called to Mr. Hainer. He began walking around the huge wagon, running his

ETHEL ROMELFANGER (left) is the calliopist whose rousing tunes overwhelm the eardrums of thousands along the parade route. Depressing the keys opens a valve, which in turn releases steam through a brass whistle.

DUKE ELLINGTON (right) hears the finer points of calliope playing from Chappie in 1966. Moments later, *Mood Indigo* could be heard for a country mile.

JUST RETURNED FROM AUSTRALIA

ROMAN HIPPODROME
3 RING CIRCUS
TWO ELEVATED STAGES,
5 CONTINENT MENAGERIE
IMPERIAL JAPANESE TROUPE

SELLS BROTHERS

COMBINED WITH HASSAN BEN ALI'S
MOORISH CARAVAN
ARABIAN NIGHTS' ENTERTAINMENT
AND SPECTACULAR
PILGRIMAGE TO MECCA

20 YEARS BEFORE THE PUBLIC.

THE SUPREME TEST OF MERIT IS SUCCESS.

THE CHILDREN'S DREAM OF FAIRY-LAND A DELIGHTFUL INTEGRAL EPISODE OF THE BEAUTIFUL
SPECTACULAR PROCESSION OF SELLS BROS' ENORMOUS UNITED SHOWS.
INTRODUCING BEAUTIFUL & APPROPRIATE CHARIOTS WITH LIVING & LAUGHABLE PERSONATIONS OF MOTHER GOOSE,
OLD WOMAN, WHO LIVED IN A SHOE, LITTLE RED RIDING HOOD, SANTA CLAUS, BLUE BEARD, CINDERELLA & ROBINSON CRUSOE.

31

THE ORIGINAL Sells Brothers 1893 lithograph introducing their collection of Children's Nursery Rhyme floats. The Barnum & Bailey circus unveiled a similar collection several years prior.

hands over the carvings saying over and over again, "What a beauty." He was awestruck.

He climbed into the back end to examine the instrument and boiler. I could hear more excited exclamations and whoops of joy from the interior.

While Fred was enjoying his toy, I poked around the wagons and spotted two more historic gems I knew Cole Bros. Circus owned. They were the "Mother Goose" float and the "Old Woman in the Shoe" float.

These two vehicles were built for the Barnum & Bailey Circus Parade in the 1880s! They were drawn by ponies and were stunning examples of the woodcarvers' craft of that era.

While I was enjoying my find, I heard Fred calling, so I went back to the

America. He was beside himself with excitement. "Let's call the owner in Chicago and try to nail this down."

After a lot of preliminary conversation, I heard Fred say, "I will give you $2,000 for the calliope. You know that wagon is in tough shape." Then he cupped his hand over the phone and said to me, "He said he has received some higher offers. You know I can't go over $2,500. What should I do?"

I said, "Fred, tell him you will give him $2,500 if he'll throw in those two little pony floats."

Then I heard Fred say, "Okay, I'll send you a check first thing Monday. He

"I poked around the wagons and found two more historic gems—the Mother Goose float and the Old Woman in the Shoe…"

turned to me, grinning from ear to ear. Suddenly his expression changed. "Hey…what do I want with those two pony floats?"

"Well," I said sheepishly, "they did help you nail down the calliope within your budget."

He nodded in agreement, then said, "I will give you one for all of your help. Find another circus nut that will give me $100 for the other one. That will help me pay for the trucking."

Then he thanked me for my assistance and asked me to write up the history of the America Steam Calliope so he could get a brochure printed.

BARNUM & BAILEY'S Old Woman in the Shoe pony float, fully restored and ready for the parade.

Circus World Museum

THE MOTHER GOOSE and Old Woman in the Shoe floats glisten in the sun aboard the Great Circus Train—surely two favorites among the children.

The America served its purpose wonderfully—promoting Cleaver-Brooks boiler products for 5 or 6 years. In that time I kept in touch with Fred. Along about 1957 or 1958 I began to suggest that someday I hoped his company would consider giving the America to the Circus World Museum, which would be opening its doors for the first time in 1959.

This is exactly what happened. The Steam Calliope arrived in Baraboo in time for the Grand Opening, on July 1.

I have a couple more anecdotes about the America Steam Calliope. One year, the day before the parade, Leonard Perkins, the Circus World Museum's maintenance man, came to me and said, "Something wrong with the cally. I can't keep the motor running."

Mel Fisher, a service engineer, was summoned. He arrived early in the evening and started checking things out. "Here is your trouble," he said, showing Leonard a carburetor full of rust flakes. The rust had broken loose in the gas tank on the jouncing train ride from Baraboo. By midnight Mel had the gas tank boiled out, clean and back to the show grounds.

At 2 a.m. Mel announced, "Let's fire her up and get up a head of steam. We want to be sure everything functions for the parade." When the boys had the steam pressure they needed, Mel pecked out *Peter, Peter Pumpkin Eater* on the calliope keyboard.

I have heard some loud calliopes in my day, but none like that one blaring in the dead of night. Of course, at 2 a.m., anybody that was awake was startled. Those that were not awake, soon were if they were within a mile or two of the show grounds!

Duke Ellington Plays Calliope

One year Schlitz brought the legendary Duke Ellington and his band to Milwaukee as a part of "Old Milwaukee Days". I met Mr. Ellington at a party. Three or four fellows were in a group talking to him. He was saying he thought he had played every kind of instrument on the face of the earth.

So I put the question to him, and he admitted he had never had the opportunity to play a steam calliope. We made a date for 11 the next morning at the show grounds.

Duke was a great sport. He readily climbed into the wagon to look over the whistles and the keyboard. He was fascinated by it all. He touched a key and nothing happened. I explained he had to push hard, as the valves under each whistle were under great pressure.

"No kitten on the keys stuff," I said to Duke.

"I gottcha," he replied. Then, grinning, he tried again. Soon he got the feel of how to play with stiff fingers, and before I realized it, Duke Ellington was belting out *Mood Indigo* on the America Steam Calliope. A memorable experience, to say the least.

The Mother Goose Float

Now lets go back to the two pony floats. A friend of mine, and a big circus fan, Roland Wilde, purchased the Old Woman in the Shoe and hauled it out to his home in Wauwatosa. Wisconsin. His young son, Walter, and his friends played around on it until 1959, when Roland Wilde donated the float to the Circus World Museum.

As for "Mother Goose", well, Fred Hainer gave that to me as a thank you. But since I did not have the money to hire a truck to haul it home, I had to pull it behind my car.

Early on a Sunday morning, my two children, Barbara and Peter, drove with me to the Cleaver-Brooks Company in Milwaukee to pick up the "Goose". We inched our way out of town and headed home on Highway 190. Out in the

SIX SORREL ponies guide the Mother Goose float through Milwaukee streets.

He said, "Sir, I won't ask you what you are towing, but do me a favor. There is a long Army convoy behind you. It would be safer if you let them pass." So I stayed where I was on the shoulder of the road.

Then came the convoy of trucks, Jeeps and other rigs all loaded with soldiers. They had a ball whistling, jeering and shouting. My children were too young to get the drift, but I was happy

"Hope those Army boys wrote home about saluting Mother Goose…"

that my wife had stayed home. The soldier boys were having fun, so we all laughed at the whole event.

A few miles later, we came up over a hill, when, to my wondering eyes should appear, but that whole darn convoy, all pulled over on the side of the

road for some reason or another. At the tail end of the Army trucks sat the same State Patrolman.

He had a big smile on his face as he waved me on, shaking his head as if to say, "I don't believe it". At 20 miles an hour, we ran the gauntlet a second time. And did we get razzed and whistled and shouted at? You better believe it.

After we had passed, Peter said, "Dad, those were neat trucks. Let's go back and do it again."

"Son, you have a lot of good ideas," I said, "but this surely isn't one of them."

I just hope all those Army boys wrote home telling about the good time they had with "Mother Goose" on a Wisconsin highway.

We cared for the "Goose" for quite a few years, but I, too, gave her to the Circus World Museum.

"Cinderella" is the only other of these floats that survived from the Barnum & Bailey 1888 collection, and hers is another story (see page 90).

country I maintained a careful speed of about 20 mph.

Soon I noticed a State Patrol car behind me. Suddenly the red light started flashing. I knew I wasn't speeding and wondered if there was a law about driving too slow. I pulled onto the shoulder and the officer approached, eyeballing Mother Goose on the way to my car.

THIS WELL-TRAVELED GOOSE paraded through major cities with the Barnum & Bailey Circus for decades, including a trip to Europe and England at the turn of the century. Top left shows the float as the author found it in an airplane hangar in 1952.

THE WALT DISNEY WAGONS

THE FIRST large group of circus wagons we went after was owned by the Walt Disney Studios in California. When Disneyland opened, Walt decided to have a one-ring circus as one of the shows. He also wanted a daily street parade. So he picked up 10 or 12 old circus wagons that were more or less deserted and rotting away, and completely restored them.

Some years later, the theme at Disneyland changed, and new entertainment was brought in. The circus wagons were put in storage. Knowing this, I wrote to Mr. Disney, suggesting the Circus World Museum would love to have them for display.

After a couple of months with no answer, I wrote another letter, even more convincing. Still no answer. I was under the impression that Mr. Disney was a friendly and compassionate person, so I felt he just never saw my letters; that they had been side-tracked by a subordinate.

I determined that the only way to get the job done was to find someone who knew Mr. Disney personally. As a result, wherever I went—Milwaukee, Chicago or Madison, meetings, parties, or lunches—I would ask at the appropriate time, "Do you know Walt Disney?" Six months later, the sun burst

Steve Hopkins

THE DISNEY COLLECTION rolled into the Baraboo train depot in the summer of 1962. The elegant Swan Bandwagon (above and below) was built for the Ringling Bros. in 1905.

Author's Collection

VOLUNTEERS Gene Traxler and Wilbur Deppe with their crews and equipment were invaluable to the museum. Here they oversee the unloading of the Disney Wagons.

Circus World Museum

WALT DISNEY (on right) admires the historic Picture Frame Cage Wagon #85, which he later donated to the Circus World Museum. The Disney "gift" of 11 parade and cage wagons was one of the largest and best maintained collections the museum ever received.

through the clouds. I was at a party in my brother Rod's home in Winnetka,

Illinois. I had been talking to George Getz Jr., who owned a huge collection of old fire engines. It was then I posed my question.

"Yes, in fact, I'm having dinner with Walt next month," he answered. You could 've knocked me over with a feather. It turned out that George was on the Board of Directors of the Santa Fe Railroad, and the railroad did a lot of business with Disney.

After I told George my problem, he said for me to write the letter to Walt. "I'll personally deliver it to him," he said. All the way back to Baraboo, my car just floated.

The next day I got a call from George. "Have you written that letter

THE PICTURE FRAME cage wagon #85 got its name because the decorative wooden framework give the appearance of two "picture frames" on each side of the wagon.

yet," he asked. "Fred Gurley, the Chairman of the Santa Fe railroad is having dinner with Walt in 2 days. He told me he would deliver it for you."

I received a call from the Studio

Manager of the Walt Disney operation 3 days later. "We are interested in your proposition and are willing to work out the details," he said.

When the wagons were ready to be

shipped, the Santa Fe sent two 80-ft.-long flatcars to the Disney studio in California. The wagons were then shipped from California to Chicago.

Upon arrival, Mr. Getz and Mr. Gurley were joined by Ernie Marsh, President of the Santa Fe, and a slew of newspaper reporters and photographers.

When all the publicity activity slowed down, Mr. Gurley asked me how I was going to get the cars from Chicago to Baraboo. I told him I would call the Chicago and North Western, as they serviced our town.

"Why don't you let me make that call," Mr. Gurley said. "If we can haul these cars 2,000 miles for you for nothing, I think the North Western can handle the last 175 miles for free." I agreed to this idea—quickly.

As things turned out, Walt Disney was friendly and compassionate. Certainly, so were all the railroads that helped out.

Disney's magnificent circus wagons rolled into Baraboo and the Circus World Museum as a gift, postage paid, in 1962.

Included in the Walt Disney collection were:

Swan Bandwagon built in 1905 for Ringling Bros.

Orchesmelchor Tableau built in 1880s for Barnum & London Circus

Cage built for Howes Great London Circus in 1920s

Sea Shell Tableau

Picture Frame Cage

Al G. Barnes Circus Ticket Wagon

Whiskers Cage built in 1880s for Barnum & Bailey

Beauty Tableau

Air Calliope

Lee Bros. Circus Baggage Wagon

Christy Bros. Circus Baggage Wagon

Now we could begin to dream seriously about staging a glorious old-fashioned circus street parade.

OFFICERS of the Santa Fe railroad presented nine of the 11 Disney Wagons, which they hauled across the country as a gift to the Circus World Museum. The Beauty Tableau and the Sea Shell Tableau in the background can be seen in the Circus Parade at top and bottom, respectively.

Allied Artists

20th Century Fox Studio

From the Big Top
To the Big Screen

MANY OLD PARADE WAGONS wound up in Hollywood, where they were used for movie props. Opposite page, top: Allied Artist's 1959 presentation of *Big Circus* starred Victor Mature, Rhonda Flemming, Vincent Price and Peter Lorre.

HENRY FONDA and Dorothy Lamour starred in *Chad Hanna* (opposite bottom), which featured the Swan Bandwagon among others.

METRO-GOLDWYN-MAYER produced *Jumbo*, starring Doris Day and Jimmy Durante, in 1963 (above). Seven old parade wagons were used in this film, including the 1883 "Whiskers" cage wagon (left). This ornate cage earned its nickname from the bearded male figures on each corner of the wagon.

GEORGE CHRISTY'S HISTORIC 'JUNK'

IN THE ERA of the 1920s, George Christy of South Houston, Texas owned a number of circuses—the largest being Christy Bros. It was a fine 20-car railroad circus.

Once I had a good visit with George at his home and asked him how many brothers he had. "Brothers!" he said, "I don't have any brothers."

"Well, George, why are there portraits of distinguished-looking men on all of your posters?"

George answered, "When my circus was growing and I was a big railroad show, I was just copying the big boys.

You know there were the Ringling Bros. Circus and the Gollmar Bros. Circus and the Sells Brothers Circus. They had legitimate brothers and I had none.

"So I went to a drugstore and looked for bottles of elixir and cough syrup and such, those that had nifty portraits on the labels. I cut out these portraits, pasted them into a nice group and sent them to the company that printed my posters."

George Christy got out of the circus business around 1930. Most of his equipment was sold to Cole Bros. Circus. But one choice cage wagon was left

behind: It was a historic beauty from the Barnum & Bailey & Hutchinson Circus of the 1880s.

On November 15, 1958, with the Circus World Museum about to open to the public, I wrote Mr. Christy to ask if he would consider giving it to our museum. Finally, in January of 1959, he responded. We were welcome to it. "It's a wreck," he warned me.

Wilbur Deppe, a Baraboo industrialist, said he would send a truck after the wagon. Wilbur's son David and Ray Broihahn went after it. In the meantime, I contacted Florence Stancliff of Hous-

Circus World Museum

DAVID DEPPE and Ray Broihahn return to Baraboo from South Houston with the venerable Barnum & Bailey Cage Wagon.

H. H. Bennett

AFTER RESTORATION, The Barnum & Bailey Cage Wagon awaits only a coat of green paint. The panel on the side of the wagon is removed while on parade or in the menagerie, and put up to protect the animals from bad weather while the circus was in route.

David and said, "Bring it back. Chappie wants that wagon."

When the loading was done, Florence said, "Boys, get in my car. We are going to get something to eat before you leave on your trip home."

The boys arrived in Baraboo April 6, 1959. David said that every 100 miles he had to stop to tighten up the tie-down ropes—the old relic kept swaying and sagging.

Then David said, "Dad, when we got through loading on that hot day, Mrs. Stancliff took us to a fancy restaurant and bought us the biggest steak dinner I ever had."

Later, I asked Wilbur for an invoice for the trucking. "Forget it," he said to me. "If a total stranger can treat my son the way that lady did, and if somebody in Texas is that interested in your museum, then I guess I can haul your wagon for you…even if it is junk."

The "junk" is now the glorious and magnificent green and gold cage wagon #61 that has been in every parade.

ton, a wonderful circus fan, whom I knew. I asked her if she would meet the boys in case they needed to know where to turn for a winch or tow truck to help load.

When the truck arrived, David looked over the wagon, then called his father.

"Dad, do you really want me to bring this piece of junk back to Baraboo?" Wilbur asked for the phone number and said, "Stay there, I'll call you back."

Then Wilbur called me and relayed the message. "But Wilbur," I pleaded, "it is *historic* junk." Wilbur called

C. P. Fox

THE CAGE WAGON was built in 1882 and used by Barnum & Bailey until 1918, then put into storage for several years. George Christy purchased it in 1925 and, some 34 years later, donated it to the Circus World Museum.

THE CARSON PIRIE SCOTT COLLECTION

"HOW did it play in Peoria?" the saying goes. When it comes to collecting ancient circus wagons, everything played admirably. Block & Kuhl was the dominant department store in Peo-

was not a bad idea. "But where can we get such wagons?" he asked.

Frank told him about the Cole Bros. Circus in Rochester, Indiana. "They do not have a street parade anymore, so

purchase washing machines, refrigerators, dish washers and other appliances. Block & Kuhl, being a department store, obviously had an inside track on this stuff. Eventually a deal was struck

THE LION AND MIRROR Bandwagon was acquired from the Cole Bros. Circus through an unusual trade: A truckload of household appliances (rare because of WWII rationing) paid for three historic wagons.

ria, Illinois during the '40s and '50s. Each year they staged a huge Christmas Parade.

A gentleman by the name of Frank Meyer worked in Block & Kuhl's maintenance department. Being an old circus fan, he suggested to his boss, H.L. Roark, that a few circus parade wagons would be a nice addition to their Christmas Parade. Mr. Roark agreed that it

their wagon collection is just laying around in storage. Maybe we can buy a few of them."

But that did not work. Zack Terrel, the Cole Bros. circus owner, was not interested in selling the wagons. "I might, however, be interested in a trade," he said.

At this time, World War II was raging and it was practically impossible to

and the wagons arrived in Peoria—paid for with a truckload of appliances.

After some fixing up and a fresh paint job, these three relics were added to their Christmas Parade:

1. The Lion & Mirror Bandwagon, originally built for the Adam Forepaugh Circus in 1878. Then, in 1890, it was sold to the Ringling Bros. and was in their parades for several years before

winding up with the Cole Bros.

2. Asia tableau built in 1903 for the Barnum & Bailey Circus.

3. France Bandwagon built in 1918 for the F.J. Spellman Motorized Circus.

When the Circus World Museum opened its doors in 1959, I felt it was a shame that these three glorious wagons were used only 1 day each year and in storage for 364 days. They should be put on display in Baraboo. So I wrote to Mr. Roark in Peoria.

But I found out that the Block & Kuhl chain of stores had been sold to Carson Pirie Scott & Company.

I was trying to think of a way to approach the company when the phone rang. It was my old friend Ray Weis-brod, a Milwaukee businessman who in his youth had played in the Ringling Bros. Circus band.

I told Ray my dilemma, and wouldn't you know it…C.V. Martin, the President of Carson Pirie Scott was a personal friend of his! Ray wrote to Mr. Martin on my behalf and things began to happen. The arrangement was sim-

JOHN PIRIE, Chairman of Carson Pirie Scott & Co., officially presents the author three parade wagons. Right, the Lion and Mirror Bandwagon in Detroit in the '30s.

THE ASIA tableau on parade in Milwaukee. The 12 wood-carved faces on the side of the wagon represent the people native to that continent.

THE FRANCE BANDWAGON was built for the F.J. Spellman Motorized Circus in 1918. It is the only wagon left from a series of 15 that each represented a country. Originally, the body of this wagon was mounted on the chassis of a truck.

ple. The Circus World Museum could have the wagons on one condition: We agreed to truck them back to Peoria every year for their Christmas Parade.

So in 1961, after their parade, three "brand-new" antiques arrived in Baraboo. For several years the museum "shared" these wagons with the department store. Then the Peoria store decided to drop them from their event, which had become more of a community affair, rather than a one-company show.

Three of the finest wagons in the collection, these gifts from Carson Pirie Scott are now permanent residents of the Circus World Museum—except for 1 week in July when they make a short trip to Milwaukee…for another parade.

A CINDERELLA STORY

IN 1951, 8 years before the museum opened, I was conducting research for a book I was writing called "A Pictorial History of the Circus Parade".

I had written to Terrell Jacobs, a famous lion and tiger trainer from that era, because I was curious about the condition of the Cinderella float which he owned.

The stunning, larger-than-life wood-carved figures of Prince Charming fitting the golden slipper on Cinderella's foot was built in the 1880s for the Barnum & Bailey Circus. It was one of nine "children's theme floats" designed by the circus.

Terrell warned me in one of his letters, "As long as I am alive, I will own Cinderella."

In 1960, after I had become Director of the Circus World Museum, I tried to locate this vehicle. Terrell Jacobs, I found, had run into hard times and no

longer owned it. Scuttlebutt told me it was in the St. Louis area, so I got in touch with my friend Brandy Johnson, who had an art studio in the city.

Brandy started snooping around like a bird dog. Trying everything, he eventually visited Guy Mullen, who owned a big pony farm outside the city.

And there she was—Cinderella—sitting in a horse pasture almost buried in

CINDERELLA arriving in Baraboo with Ernie Zimmerly, the head of the wagon shop, and the Schwartz truck driver that brought her to Wisconsin from Missouri.

A FEW of the components of the throne and body of Cinderella (above). This wonderful parade float was saved from a rotting death in the nick of time. The paint was practically gone, exposing the wood to the elements. Coating the wood with boiled linseed oil saturates the pores and prevents further decomposition. Then the wood is treated with primer, and finally paint.

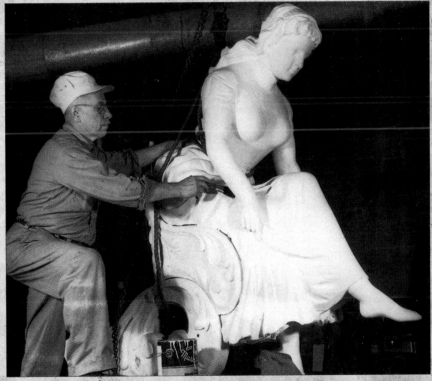

ERNIE ZIMMERLY carefully lowers the treated and restored Cinderella carving onto the wagon undercarriage (right).

THE CINDERELLA pony float (below) followed by Mother Goose (background) in Hamburg, Germany. This parade was part of Barnum & Bailey's 1900 European tour.

THE ELEGANT symmetry of this classic wood carving make the Cinderella float one of the finest artistic creations in circus history.

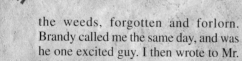

the weeds, forgotten and forlorn. Brandy called me the same day, and was he one excited guy. I then wrote to Mr. Mullen and expressed a great desire to meet with him.

Guy Mullen turned out to be a fascinating person and very interested in the circus. We discovered that Mullen's family traced back to the Gentrys who operated a number of Dog and Pony

Shows many years back.

I explained the mission of the Circus World Museum to Guy, and, of course, showed him some photographs, one of which illustrated an entire wall of very large old circus posters. Prominent in the display was an enormous "Gentry Bros. Famous Shows" poster that he thought was quite beautiful.

Then Guy said, "In addition to the

Cinderella float, I also have an old cage wagon you might want to examine." He took us over to an old shed and there, up along one side, sat a decrepit old cage wagon. I didn't even recognize it.

"The corner carvings were removed years ago and I have them stored in one of my buildings. You can have them, too," Guy said.

When I saw the wood carvings, I

knew immediately we had a gem—it was the leopard cage wagon from the Sells Floto Circus.

In addition, Guy had a special cart designed to be pulled by a llama. (This, we later determined, had been with the Hagenbeck-Wallace Circus). Guy gen-

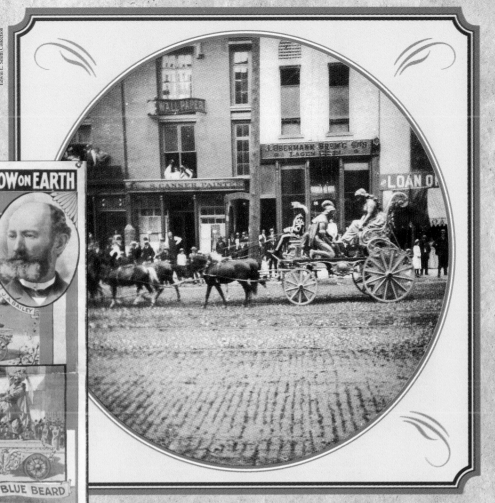

THE CINDERELLA FLOAT made its first (but not last!) parade appearance in Milwaukee in 1888. This vehicle was typically drawn by six black ponies.

THIS ORIGINAL lithograph from the late 1880s (left) introduced Barnum & Bailey's "Childhood's Fairyland". A collection of nine pony floats that celebrated various children's themes, these wagons represent some prime examples of the wood-carving craft. Three of these historic gems have survived the century and are displayed in the Circus World Museum.

erously donated these five relics to the Circus World Museum.

As we were sitting around having a cup of coffee, I asked Guy how these historic gems happened to end up on his pony farm. He said, "Terrell Jacobs and his little circus were playing in St. Louis. Terrell called me and explained he needed $500 to pay a few bills in order to get out of town."

"I asked what he had for collateral on such a loan. He mentioned these three wagons. I told him to bring them out and I would loan him the $500. That was years ago and I haven't seen hide nor hair of him since."

So one man gathers what another man spills, I guess you could say. Cinderella and the rest of the historic vehicles arrived at the Circus World Museum on October 8, 1961, and have been highlights of the parade ever since.

THE WILD WEST WAGONS

COLORFUL WAGON has carried three different kinds of musical instruments throughout its long career. Built in 1902 as a steam calliope, it now contains a band organ—a mechanical instrument involving a perforated paper roll.

THE WILD WEST SHOWS of the late 1800s and early 1900s were truly something to behold. Sort of a cross between the circus and a rodeo, they featured incredible horsemanship, rope tricks, acrobatics and battle reenactments between the "Cavalry" and the "Indians".

These shows were similar to the circus in that they traveled by rail and staged tremendous street parades. As a result they featured some beautiful wagons.

When the wagons and railroad cars of the defunct 101 Ranch Wild West show were put up for auction, Bill Hames, a Fort Worth carnival owner, was on hand to acquire some of this equipment.

Three circus parade wagons had intrigued him: The Great Britain Bandwagon, Pawnee Bill's Bandwagon and a Cole Bros. Calliope Wagon. All three dated back to the early 1900s.

In 1958 I wrote to Bill Hames about these wagons. I knew they were stunning examples of American folk art.

As you might guess, I was interested in acquiring them for the museum. But I did not receive an answer. In May of 1960, after becoming Director of the museum, I wrote to him again...still no answer.

Then I heard the old gentleman had passed away in June; so I wrote to his son, Frank. He, in turn, suggested I contact their attorney, Jack C. Wessler. Mr.

> *"A cross between the circus and a rodeo, Wild West shows featured incredible horsemanship and acrobatics..."*

Wessler was the executor of the estate. He indicated that while something might be worked out, it was much too early to make a decision.

I was concerned that as an unknown in little old Baraboo, I might get lost in the cracks. So I enlisted the services of Wisconsin Senators Alexander Wiley

and Bill Proxmire. They sent letters to Mr. Wessler indicating their deep interest in the historic wagons. Senator Wiley even wrote to Texas Senator Lyndon B. Johnson expressing Wisconsin's desire to preserve circus history.

But a few months later, the Hames family informed me they wanted to keep the wagons. That didn't stop me.

In March 1961 I wrote Theo Ledel, the partner of the late Bill Hames. He, too, loved these historic wagons, and soon realized that Ft. Worth was not the place for them. I kept in contact with Theo, until finally, he said, "Come on down to Texas and we'll talk it over."

On August 1 I visited with Mr. Wessler and Mr. Ledel. I did not get any commitments, but I felt like I made a good case for the museum. "We've been up to our necks in letters from senators and everybody else," Mr. Wessler charged. "I don't know why these wagons are so important to everyone, but we won't forget you, Mr. Fox."

In May I received a letter from Theo Ledel. "The Hames family has been

THE PAWNEE BILL BANDWAGON on parade with the 101 Ranch Wild West show in 1920.

considering your offer to have the wagons preserved and put on display. There is going to be a meeting with all the heirs of the estate on May 31, here in Fort Worth. It might be in your best interest to attend."

When I arrived in Fort Worth the decision had already been made! The family agreed to loan us all the wagons—until the complicated estate was finalized. Then the wagons would be appraised and officially presented to the Circus World Museum. I was extremely pleased, and caught myself daydreaming, visualizing the wagons after a trip through our restoration shop.

The acquisition of the wagons was secure but another momentous problem existed: transporting the wagons back to Baraboo. The museum had no budget to speak of at all. In fact, the Historical Society frowned on the wagon collection altogether. "Where are you going to put them? You already have 12, why do you need more?" they said.

In 1962 the Circus World Museum was only in its third year of existence. The Great Circus Parade did not even exist. It was nearly impossible to expect a company to pay the freight from Ft.

BUILT IN 1903, the Pawnee Bill Bandwagon is one of the finest examples of American folk art in existence. The mural on the side of the wagon depicts the arrival of Columbus in the new world.

THE GREAT BRITAIN BANDWAGON is another stunning example of American folk art, this time paying tribute to Britain, with a wood-carved emblem of John Bull. Below, the same wagon, nearly 70 years earlier (the 1920s) with the 101 Ranch Wild West show.

Worth to Baraboo on some decrepit, ancient wagons.

But that is exactly what happened. Back in Baraboo, I called on my friend Joe Johnson, who in turned called Phillip Nason, the President of First National Bank. As it turned out, Phil had a connection with the Chicago Burlington

> *"Everything was falling into place. I went back to Ft. Worth to begin loading the wagons..."*

and Quincy Railroad. This railroad owned miles of track in both Wisconsin and Texas.

I was advised to meet with a Mr. J.J. Alm, the Executive Assistant to the President of the railroad. Mr. Alm was very cordial, and wouldn't you know it, turned out to be a great fan of the

READY TO ROLL from Ft. Worth, Texas to Baraboo are flatcars from the Bill Hames Carnival, loaded with the seven historic parade wagons donated by the Hames family.

circus. He was extremely interested in this unusual shipment and happy to be involved.

Everything was falling into place. On September 10, 1962 I went back to Ft. Worth to load the wagons. With Theo Ledel's assistance, we loaded, chocked and tied down these wagons:

PAWNEE BILL BANDWAGON

GREAT BRITAIN BANDWAGON

SELLS & DOWNS STEAM CALLIOPE WAGON

101 RANCH WILD WEST BAGGAGE WAGON

Then Theo said, "You have the transport space, so why not take three carnival wagons also." We did. The total evaluation by an appraisal company was almost $150,000.

A call was made to the railroad to pick up the loaded flatcars, and the wagons were on their way to the museum!

I had about 3 hours to kill before my flight departed, so I decided to go over to the Amon Carter Museum of Western Art. I introduced myself to the Director and he seemed quite interested in Wisconsin's Circus World Museum.

"What brings you to Ft. Worth?" he asked. When I explained my mission he exclaimed, "Don't tell me that this includes the Pawnee Bill Bandwagon?"

When I told him it did, he exclaimed, "That magnificent wagon is one of the greatest examples of American folk art in existence. I have had my eye on it for years!"

"Gee," I said. "I sure am sorry."

Meanwhile, I was grateful that I hadn't visited this gentleman when I was in town that May. He could have upset the whole applecart.

On October 3, 1962 the two antique flatcars, brimming with their historic load, pulled into Baraboo. After restoration, the wagons were absolutely breathtaking—even better than my daydreams had suggested.

THEO LEDEL (right) was the right-hand man to legendary showman Bill Hames for over 40 years. Theo was instrumental in working out the details in donating Hames' wagon collection to the museum.

UNIVERSAL STUDIO WAGONS

THE BARNUM & BAILEY CAGE WAGON #83 is the sole survivor from a 1915 series of wagons that featured landscape paintings on the side.

THE BIG RAILROAD CIRCUS, Hagenbeck-Wallace, went out of business in 1938—the tail end of the Depression years. All of their equipment was sold and dispersed to various circuses and collectors. Five of these historic wagons wound up at the Universal Studios in Los Angeles, where they were used as props for circus movies.

These were some very choice wagons, so in 1963 I made an appointment to visit with the Studio Manager. When I got to Universal, he had one of his men take me through the grounds in a small motorized vehicle. We wound our way through a variety of cities, country villages, and old Western towns. They were phony, of course, but looked real from the front.

As we rounded a corner, we suddenly came face-to-face with what

THE FAIRY TALES TABLEAU, from the Hagenbeck-Wallace Circus, features Peter Pumpkin Eater on one side and Little Red Riding Hood on the other. This enormous wagon stretches almost 20 feet long, is 12 feet high and weighs approximately 4 tons.

CAL AND MAIDA BERGNER (at work below) were in charge of all of the finishing painting, stripping and lettering for the museum's wagons and railroad cars during the '60s.

appeared to be a gigantic stone castle, complete with turrets, a moat and a drawbridge. Lined up in front, like automobiles in a row, were the five circus wagons…and what beauties they were.

I decided then and there this was no place for these historic gems. They showing that the studio could easily build proper sized wagon bodies. All he needed was the running gear. Then they could change bodies to emulate the circus, a medicine show or a minstrel show. The wagons would look better and be easier to handle. He shook his tax deduction. Obviously, I was talking to the wrong man.

When I got to Milwaukee I called Joe Johnson. He was a circus buff and an old friend that had helped me out many times. I explained my failure in detail and added, "How can we find

looked sadly out of place in "King Arthur's Court."

I got out of the cart and examined them closely—revelling in their fine condition. Then I measured their dimensions. Mentally, however, I was sizing up my chances of getting a donation out of the Studio.

"No," the Studio Manager said when I popped the question. Just a flat "no".

I tried to explain the historic significance of the wagons. I told him that these were some of the most massive railroad circus wagons ever built—they looked ridiculous being used as props for small "movie" circuses.

Quickly, I made some sketches, head. "Where am I going to get the running gear?" he asked.

I told him we had such gear at the Circus World Museum that we could ship to him.

My sales pitch wasn't working. I saved the best for last. "With the approval of an appraisal company, Universal might be eligible for a nice tax deduction," I offered.

"We are happy with things the way they are," was his final answer.

So I flew back to Wisconsin and thought about two things. First, the Studio Manager had no desire to contribute to the museum and preserve history. Second, he did not even care about the out who owns Universal Studios? If we can get to the top man, maybe I would have a chance."

In a minute or two Joe was talking on the telephone—explaining the situation. "Who is the top guy?" I heard him ask. "Okay, thank you very much." When Joe hung up he explained that he had been talking to the President of a large bank in New York.

Universal Studios, Joe said, was part of a conglomerate that included eight big recording companies and others. He handed me the name and address of the top guy and smiled. "Good luck, Chap… and let me know how you come out."

I recall that I sent my letter to New York on a Thursday. The following Monday I got a phone call from the Studio Manager at Universal in Los Angeles—the same gent I had visited with when I was out there!

"Fox, you son of a gun, what are you doing to me?" he demanded. He was a little perturbed. Yet he informed me that he had been instructed to hand the wagons over to the museum! So, amicably, we discussed all of the details and made the shipping arrangements.

Then, as I had promised, the Circus World Museum sent four wagon under-carriages to Los Angeles. And shortly thereafter, five historic circus wagons

---

"Five historic circus wagons came rolling into Baraboo—a gift from Universal Studios..."

---

came rolling into Baraboo—a gift from Universal Studios.

After a run through the restoration shop, the wagons found their way into another "castle," the Circus World Museum, and have complemented the Great Circus Parade every year since their arrival in 1963. The five wagons are:

1. Sells-Floto Circus: Cage Wagon #19
2. Hagenbeck-Wallace Circus: Cage Wagon #25
3. Hagenbeck-Wallace Circus: Fairy Tale Tableau #75 (Peter Pumpkin Eater on one side and Little Red Riding Hood on the other)
4. Barnum & Bailey Circus: Cage Wagon #83
5. Hagenbeck-Wallace Circus: Stringer Wagon #101.

THE LOUIS GOEBEL COLLECTION

WHEN THE Hagenbeck-Wallace Circus called it quits in 1938, a man named Louis Goebel was on hand to purchase the defunct circus. An animal importer and exporter, Louis purchased the circus in order to obtain all of the menagerie animals.

Since his purchase also provided him with many classic parade and baggage wagons, he went into the business of leasing circus equipment to the movie studios.

On December 1, 1960, my first year as Director of the Circus World Muse-um, I wrote to Mr. Goebel to inquire about the wagons. He answered that he only owned one ticket wagon and wanted to keep it. The other wagons had been sold to his neighbors who operated the "Jungleland Compound".

I continued to keep in touch with Mr. Goebel, as he was interested in our museum. Late in January of 1961, he informed me that he had repossessed all of his wagons. More letters were exchanged. In May, Louis said he would let me know within a few weeks what he planned to do with his collection.

Then I contacted my friend, Frank Whitbeck in Los Angeles. He and Louis were old friends from the movie industry. Frank went to see Louis on my behalf, and before you knew it, the museum received wagon #91 as a gift.

This visit broke the ice and I soon found out that Louis Goebel was a genuinely fine person—warm and friendly. In April 1963, the Charging Tiger Tableau #11 arrived in Baraboo on a flatbed truck—another gift!

When the truck driver arrived, he was shaking his head in disbelief. "Back

LOUIS GOEBEL'S gift of 13 historic wagons was the largest single donation the museum ever received. The massive Charging Tiger tableau was the first to arrive.

THE ROBBINS BROS. Cross Cage Wagon used to carry parrots, macaws and other small animals. Wagons of this dimension earned their name because they could be loaded "crosswise" on the flatcar to save linear space.

in California I had to take the wheels off this wagon and strap them down to the bed," he said. "It was just too tall to ride steady. Well, 'round Omaha, I pulled into a truck stop for some lunch. I checked my cargo and noticed I was only carrying three wheels!"

I started to feel dizzy. This was a massive 300-pound wheel built by St. Mary's Wheel and Spoke Company—decades out of business. It was simply irreplaceable.

"So I backtracked my route," the truck driver explained, "halfway through the state of Nebraska...and there she was, laying alongside the highway!"

I let out a sigh of relief. A three-wheeled wagon wouldn't have been much good to anyone—so we had a close call.

In October 1963 I went to California and visited with Louis Goebel. What I determined quickly was that Louis and his wife, Kathy, were truly interested in what we were doing in Baraboo. We developed a very close relationship.

Finally, in May of 1965, Louie wrote me and asked if we could get the wagons appraised. We contacted an appraisal company in Milwaukee, and

they assigned their "fine arts" man to the job.

When the IRS accepted the appraisal, I invited Mr. and Mrs. Goebel to Baraboo. I wanted to prove to them that their collection would be in good hands—these wagons meant an awful lot to them.

The Goebel's were most impressed, not only with the Circus World Museum, but with the work our wagon shop

---

" It took a lot of patience, but most important, the building of friendship and trust..."

---

had done in restoring the many circus wagons in the collection.

In conversation, I told Louie about the close call we had with the wagon wheel in Nebraska. He responded by saying that he knew a man by the name of Jefferies who was going to build a fence with old wagon wheels .

It turned out that Mr. Jefferies had 10 St. Marys wheels in perfect condition—the same type that our truck-driving friend had almost lost! Jefferies said

he would trade these wheels with the museum for 10 extremely large 14-spoke lumber wagon wheels we had.

With this trade complete, the 10 circus wheels, along with Louie Goebel's 13 Hagenbeck-Wallace wagons, were loaded onto low-boy trailers and trucked off to Baraboo. They arrived in December of 1965.

Two of them were cage wagons. One was a ticket wagon that we later used as a press office at the show grounds. A couple were tableau wagons and at least five were large baggage wagons that we used for storing the parade wardrobe.

The Louis Goebel collection was the largest number of wagons we ever received at one time. It took a lot of patience, but most important, the building of friendship and trust.

My friend Louis Goebel has since died, but as I write this, I mention that in the last few years his family has visited the Circus World Museum on two occasions.

It is always such a pleasure to show them the wonderful historic wagons they gave us, as they realize that their wagons are being enjoyed by all of America.

THE GOLDEN AGE OF CHIVALRY

THE GOLDEN AGE OF CHIVALRY was built in the winter of 1902-03 for the Barnum & Bailey Circus—hand-carved by the craftsmen at the Sebastian Wagon Works in New York City.

IT TOOK 10 mighty long years to acquire this spectacular circus parade wagon. It also took some mighty good friends, a little luck and an awful lot of perseverance.

The Golden Age of Chivalry was built in the winter of 1902-03 for the Barnum & Bailey Circus by the Sebastian Wagon Works in New York City. Its sole use was to parade down the main street in each show town. In other words, it did not carry any baggage in its interior.

My first letter to Mr. Alberto Garganigo, the man who owned the vehicle, was in 1958, 1 year before the Circus World Museum opened its doors. Mr. Garganigo owned and operated a museum of transportation in Princeton, Massachusetts. Basically, it specialized in antique automobiles.

He simply was not interested in letting go of the wagons. I wrote him again —3 years later—and received the same answer. Mr. Garganigo passed away in

1961. So I contacted his brother, who was the executor of the estate.

In September of 1963 I visited with him and found him to be very much interested in the possibility of giving the vehicle to the Circus World Museum. In 1964 I discovered that the family was trying to sell the entire collection intact, but they might hold out the Golden Age of Chivalry.

Then, in 1965 I heard that the entire collection had been sold—lock, stock, and "Chivalry" to a Mr. Gene Zimmerman of Harrisburg, Pennsylvania. I was back to square one.

Gene Zimmerman, I found out, owned a series of very fine motels in the area. His hobby was collecting antique cars —and the acquisition of the entire Garganigo Museum made him a very prestigious collector.

I wrote to Mr. Zimmerman suggesting the Chivalry horse drawn wagon was a bit incongruous in a museum of antique autos. I guess my letter came a little too soon after his major acquisition. He answered that he was not going to sell any part of the collection. I waited until the new year and wrote Mr. Zimmerman again. The answer was the same.

In July 1966 I called him. He was very pleasant and promised that if he decided to sell, he would give the museum a call. Then he added that he would *trade* the

---

> *"He would trade the wagon for an automobile —either a pre-1915 Rolls Royce or a Duesenberg."*

---

circus wagon for a couple of rare automobiles he had been looking for.

The autos he wanted were a Dusenberg J and a pre-1915 Rolls Royce. These cars were not exactly Model T's—I had my work cut out for me.

Back in Milwaukee, I contacted Bill Wright and Kip Stevens, who were collectors of old cars. With their help, I got to the experts in this field and began to accumulate a sizable list of antique automobile owners.

By April 1967, I was writing letters all over the country to people who owned a Dusenberg J or a pre-1915 Rolls Royce. Every letter I wrote, I sent a blind copy to Mr. Zimmerman. He would at least know I was working on our unusual deal.

Eventually, my friend Bill Wright found a 1902 Franklin in beautiful condition. I had a brainstorm and wrote Harrah's in Reno, who might have a Dusenberg.

Maybe they would want the 1902 Franklin, and we could work a three-way trade: Bill Wright's Franklin for a Harrah's Dusenberg; and Harrah's Dusenberg for the Chivalry wagon, which would go to our friend Bill Wright.

Harrah's checked into the Franklin,

"SPINE-TINGLING" PAINT JOB completed the restoration of the Golden Age of Chivalry. When it arrived in Baraboo in 1967, it was in "pretty rough shape". Expert wood-carvers were called in to repair the chipped pieces and treat the wood.

CREWMEN of the Circus World Museum are loading the Chivalry wagon onto the Circus Train with Percheron draft horses. The journey to Milwaukee lies ahead.

LADY GUINEVERE, portrayed by Patty Brash, rides the two-headed dragon. Has she tamed this magnificent beast?

which interested them very much. But then they wrote back: They had to have a 1903 model, not a 1902. Holy mackerel, of such slight links is the chain of life composed!

I called Mr. Zimmerman again and he said, "Your time is running out, Fox. Give me your best cash offer." So once again, I went to Harrisburg.

Mr. Zimmerman said, "I want $12,000 cash on the barrel head and I will give you 30 days. If I do not hear from you, I am pulling the wagon into my new building…and there she will stay."

In the file at the Circus World Museum covering the Golden Age of Chivalry, I have recently found a scribbled note I wrote to myself in 1967. "This can't be the final answer. How can I get this wagon to Baraboo? There have to be more stones to kick over."

On my way home from Pennsylvania, all kinds of ideas were whirling through my mind. One, in particular, I thought had possibilities: Marshall Field & Co. was beginning to build quite a name in Wisconsin and might appreciate the opportunity to help out the Great Circus Parade.

I contacted an old friend, Stanley Grannis, who lived at Oconomowoc Lake. I knew Jerry Sivige, the President of Marshall Field's, also owned a home on Oconomowoc Lake. Stan said, "Yes, I know him, he is here every weekend. I will invite Jerry over for dinner and that will give you an opportunity to talk to him".

Stan arranged a small dinner party at his home. In the course of the evening, I explained my plight to Mr. Sivige. He was very much interested in the idea, and when our conversation ended he said, "Can you be in my office in Chicago next Tuesday at 9 a.m.?"

At the appointed time, I was in his office with a folder full of photos of this spectacular wagon. We went over the entire story again. Then Mr. Sivige called in his secretary and asked her to have a check made out to Gene Zimmerman for $12,000, which he then gave to me.

Mr. Sivige thanked me for giving Marshall Field this opportunity, and speechless, I shook his hand.

There were only 2 days left on Mr. Zimmerman's 30-day deadline. When I walked into his office I did not mess around talking about the weather and my flight. I just handed him the check.

Mr. Zimmerman looked it over, then said, "Marshall Field, huh? I have heard of them. I guess this check is good." With that, he extended his hand across his desk. "The wagon is all yours."

The Golden Age of Chivalry arrived in Baraboo October 23, 1967. "Ten long years," I say to myself every time I look at this tremendous wagon—and it all was worthwhile.

CROWD FAVORITE. The Golden Age of Chivalry has delighted audiences since its first appearance in the Great Circus Parade in 1968. Every year nearly 750,000 spectators gather to feast their eyes on glorious sights such as this one.

THE ENGLISH WAGONS

IN THE SUMMER of 1968, a very interesting visitor came into my office. A man named Hugo Zeiter—he was in the U.S. Army and stationed in Okinawa, Japan. He was a big fan of the circus, so on his way home to Illinois, he

on the road or at their winter quarters. On one of his jaunts he said he remembered seeing some very old, beautifully wood-carved circus wagons stored in a shed.

I perked up considerably, and, of course, asked Hugo where he saw this

hoping to further jog his memory.

Finally, Hugo said, "When I get home in a few days I'll see if I can find the negatives of the photos I took. Maybe that will help me remember."

Three weeks later, Hugo wrote me a

TEETERING SHED in Tiffield, England was discovered by an American soldier during WWII. He presented a photograph like this one to the Circus World Museum 25 years later, in 1968. After an intensive search, the shed was again located, and 11 historic masterpieces were found inside, unmoved since 1918.

stopped by to visit the Circus World Museum.

In the course of our conversation, Hugo told me that he was stationed in England during World War II. Every time he had a free weekend, he would visit one of the English circuses—either

sight! "Well…you know that was 25 years ago…" he stammered. "I don't quite remember."

The more he described what he *did* remember, the more I persisted in my questioning. I must have listed every circus in England and its hometown,

letter. He said that he still could not remember where he saw these old wagons. He did, however, enclose a set of photos of the wagons he saw.

The photos were very dim, obviously taken on an overcast day, of wagons inside an old wooden shed. But enough

feet in the air. While the show is en route, though, traveling over country roads, the upper section is lowered so the wagon is not top-heavy.

Some of the large English circuses owned telescoping tableau wagons like this and used them in the era of 1860 up to probably World War I.

Seeing these photos, and then realizing Hugo could not remember where he took them, just about drove me nuts. I couldn't stand it.

I had a friend in England named Jack Niblett, who was a big circus buff. Jack had been to the Circus World Museum, so he knew what we were all about. I wrote to Jack and told him Hugo's story. We offered to pay his expenses if he could visit various circus winter quarters in the hopes of finding these wagons.

Jack wrote back in words to this effect, "I have scoured the English countryside for years, and so have a great many other circus fans. I am sorry to report that there just aren't any parade wagons left."

Nonetheless, I wrote Jack back and

THE GLADIATOR TABLEAU waited its turn in the wagon restoration shop. Master wood-carvers were assigned the monumental task of repairing the elaborate sculpting. Below, a close-up of some of the wood-carved figures on the tableau. See finished wagon on the next page.

detail could be seen to indicate some classic historic beauties. The wood carving was unbelievable!

It appeared to me that one or maybe two of the wagons might be what we call a telescoping tableau. A telescoping tableau means that the upper portion of the wagon can be cranked down into the lower portion. When in a street parade, the upper portion towers 18, maybe 20

BUILT ABOUT 1865, the Gladiator Telescoping Tableau was used by the Sir Robert Fossett Circus. It is one of the oldest and certainly most fascinating wagons in the Circus World Museum's collection.

asked him to give it one more shot. I explained what he already realized—if these wagons actually existed—we could claim a veritable gold mine of historic artifacts. So Jack agreed to search, once more.

A few weeks later, I received a letter from England. I opened it with fumbling and trembling hands.

"I have found them," it said, and I about fell off my chair! In his letter, Jack explained that he had gone to

Northampton, the winter quarters of the Sir Robert Fossett Circus. The show was on the road, but he talked to an old caretaker. Jack found out that before the Circus wintered in Northampton—they had used the old family homestead at Tiffield, which was about 10 miles away.

It was there that Jack located the circus wagons. They had not rolled a wheel since Hugo Zeiter had photographed them in 1943.

My first inclination was to telephone the Circus owner, whom I found out was Bailey Fossett. His family had been in the circus business since the time of Napoleon. But a phone call was silly, as the show was still on its summer tour.

So I wrote Mr. Fossett a long letter, explaining what the Circus World Museum was all about. I enclosed a big packet of photographs. When Mr. Fossett came back to his winter quarters and read my letter, he would at least

THE TWIN LION Telescoping Tableau, straight off the freight ship from England in 1969, will soon see some better days. (The top third of the wagon has been lowered into the body.)

know who I was. Sure enough, when I called him in November, he went on and on about the wonderful Circus World Museum.

"Mr. Fossett," I interrupted, "I understand you have a few old circus parade wagons at your farm in Tiffield."

"Yes, we do," he answered, "but I am embarrassed to report that they are in quite a pathetic condition."

"If I come over to Northampton, would you consider talking to me about acquiring a couple for our museum?" I asked gingerly.

"Certainly," he said, "I would be delighted to meet you, Mr. Fox."

A month later, I was in Northampton. Bailey Fossett picked me up at my hotel and we drove through the countryside. It was a cold, drizzly morning, but I did not mind. Tiffield was a quaint, picturesque town…beautiful stone walls along the road and lovely homes in the hills.

Mr. Fossett explained that his family had lived here for years—farming the land and operating the circus. As their Circus grew, they needed a larger winter quarters, so they had moved to Northampton.

Not far past the town, we turned and drove down a long, winding driveway. I could see Mr. Fossett's lovely stone house in the distance and a stone barn with arched doorways. Mr. Fosset parked the car. "We will have to walk from here. It is too muddy to drive."

So we squished down the road. As we came around the rear of the barn, I discovered a beaten pole shed with a sheet metal roof. Frayed remnants of canvas around the corners were all that

was left of the walls. I crouched down and peered into the dark shed. There they were: The traces of several rare, historic and incredible circus parade wagons. I was speechless. I thought

FULLY RESTORED and parading in Milwaukee, the Twin Lion Tableau is able to "telescope" up to 17 feet tall with the turn of a crank. Its three-tiered wedding-cake design is a unique and rare feature among circus wagons.

back to Hugo—only a few months ago he had showed me this very picture.

I imagined him, an American soldier, stumbling onto this very sight in the middle of WWII. Then I pictured the wagons as they must have looked on the streets of London in the 1860s. I simply could not believe my eyes.

Suddenly, Mr. Fossett's voice brought me out of my daze. He was apologizing for their condition.

"You know, they are all horse-drawn wagons. Since we began moving our circus on trucks, we have had no use for them. But I couldn't stand to part with the wagons. My late grandfather would not have approved. He used to go to auctions and buy all sorts of old circus equipment.

"I think a few of these wagons came from Lord George Sanger's Circus," he continued. "You know, George Sanger was no more a Lord than you or I. But it sounded good. My grandfather got the drift, and to this day our show is called the Sir Robert Fossett Circus."

"Mr. Fossett," I had to interrupt, "how long have these wagons been here?"

"My Father once told me that during World War I, probably 1917 or 1918, the Army confiscated all our horses. This, in effect, put our show out of business as we moved from town to town with horsepower. So everything was put in storage. After the war, our circus switched to trucks. So here the wagons have sat."

"How many of the wagons do you think you would want?" Mr. Fossett then asked.

"Well, Sir," I said, "that all depends on how much money you want for them...I'm on a pretty tight budget. I will have to raise the money."

"Oh, Mr. Fox, these wagons are not for sale." he announced. "They are cherished family heirlooms."

Well, I'll tell you, my heart sank right down into the mud. One thought raced through my head: Then what in the world am I doing here?

Mr. Fossett continued, "We would like to *give* them to you, however."

Oh, now the sun was shining. My heart felt like a yo-yo. A quick count told me there were eight or 10 wagons in that shed.

Before I made this trip, I had explained to Ben Barkin the new dimension the English wagons would bring to our parade. But we had talked about adding one or two. Oh, how I wished Ben was standing in the mud with me.

Now, Mr. Fossett was saying, "How

Author's Photo

THE ROYAL Italian Circus bandwagon (above) was found in the Tiffield shed along with the 10 English circus wagons—only this one didn't quite make it under the roof. It got left out in the cold for more than 50 years. It took over 1 year to restore some of the Tiffield wagons. Much of the wood had to be replaced, but all of the wood carvings on the wagon at left are original.

C.P. Fox

THE ORNATE DOLPHIN TABLEAU needs only a hitch and driver to join in on the parade fun (left). Each wagon arrived in the Port of Milwaukee in a separate box (at right), including a crate of "wood chips", scraped from the floor of the shed and later used to authentically restore the wood carvings.

many do you want." I thought to myself: Strike while the iron is hot. "We will take them all," I said.

We wiggled between the tightly packed wagons and I was able to confirm that there were 11 in all; two of which were the absolutely sensational telescoping tableaux—famous wagons that I had read about for years.

Mr. Fossett then said, "Let's go back home and have a spot of tea. I want you to meet my sister, Mary. She and I own and operate our circus together."

Mary turned out to be a charming person, and she too apologized for the condition of the wagons. They said they simply could not afford to keep them in shape.

"The Circus World Museum should have all of the wagons," they agreed. "That will please us greatly."

The next day we contacted an export company and they sent their men out to Tiffield to examine the cargo. "We will send our lorries out here and bring all the wagons into our shop," they explained. "After they are properly boxed, we will haul them to London and put them on a ship."

"Could you please rake the earthen floor after you remove the wagons from the pole barn?" I asked. "We want to

preserve all the bits and pieces of wood carving on the wagons."

With that, I thanked the Fossetts profusely and flew back to the States.

Six months later, a German freight ship sailed from the Atlantic into the Great Lakes and brought our precious

---

"A German freight ship sailed from the Atlantic into the Great Lakes and brought our precious cargo directly into Milwaukee's port...."

---

cargo directly to Milwaukee's port. The boxes were then loaded onto flatcars and sent off to Baraboo.

When I was in the Milwaukee port office finalizing the paperwork, I was asked for the U.S. Custom papers. "Have you paid the import duty on these wagons?" the Port authority asked.

That detail had never entered my head. I told him I had not. "No problem," he said. "Just go over there, declare the value, and they will tell you the duty."

A duty meant money; yet he said "no problem". Oh boy, I knew differently. I

went to the U.S. Custom office on Michigan Avenue and introduced myself to the top man.

"Are you the fellows that put on the Circus Parade every summer?" he asked. "Yes, Sir," I said. For the next 10 minutes he told me how he and his family watched it every year; where they sat; how they planned; how they photographed. I just let him talk on. Finally he said, "By the way, what can I do for you, Mr. Fox?"

So I told him about our shipment from England. I said these were ancient, decrepit wagons.

"Wait a minute. Did you say these wagons were ancient? You know anything over 100 years old is classed as an antique. There's no duty on antiques."

I showed him some photos of two of the wagons in a parade in England in 1865. "That makes them 104 years old," he said, "so there is no duty."

With all the papers in order, the shipment was cleared. The C&NW Railroad picked up the loaded flatcars and delivered them to the Circus World Museum in June 1969.

By this time, word had gotten around that we had the English wagons. So we hauled two or three over to the museum courtyard for our guests to see.

That fall, all our efforts were at restoring these wagons. Master woodcarvers Bill Thallmeyer and Joe Horvat were contracted to replace the missing parts. Marv Gauger, the museum's wagon master, and his crew tackled the wagons' restoration.

The Joseph Schlitz Brewing Co. paid for the entire restoration of all 11 English wagons, which included the Royal Mail Coach; the Temple Tableau; Gladiator and Twin Lion Tableaux (telescoping); the Star Tableau; Dolphin Tableau; the Royal Italian bandwagon and others.

Bob Uihlein graciously invited Bailey and Mary Fossett to come to Milwaukee at his expense to see the Great Circus Parade and the restoration of the glorious wagons they gave the Circus World Museum. Sadly, they answered that they would be on the road with their circus and just could not get away at this busy time.

As the English wagons paraded down the Milwaukee streets on the Fourth of July in 1970, I was struck by the historical irony.

The wagons had been built during the Civil War, then rendered powerless as the horses that pulled them were called into WWI. When the automobile was invented, they were deemed unnecessary.

They withstood over 100 years of changing seasons, only to journey to America and be resurrected back to their original glorious condition.

Let's hope they stay with us for another 100 years…or more.

BAND OF CLOWNS rides on the Italian Bandwagon (below).

THE ENGLISH WAGONS in the Great Circus Parade: Above— The Star Tableau, featuring the Ringling Bros. and Barnum & Bailey's world-famous Unicorn. Six beautifully matched Percheron draft horses pull the Twin Lion Tableau (below). Cleopatra, played by Donna Strong, rides aboard the luxurious Temple Tableau (below right).

The Legendary
Bell Wagon Rings On

THE CREW of Moeller Wagon Works stand proudly before the finished Bell Wagon in 1892. Second from the left is Corwin Moeller. Henry Jr. is fourth from left, and on his left is their father, Henry Moeller Sr. Below, Henry Jr. in the 1950s.

When the Ringling Bros. Bell Wagon rolls through the Great Circus Parade, crowds are gazing at what is perhaps the most talked-about wagon in circus history.

All circus lingo aside, the Bell Wagon is a masterpiece. Not just from a visual standpoint, though for appearance alone, this wagon is something to behold. Nine massive bronze bells are mounted on a brilliant crimson frame, and glorious gold wood carvings of noble diety-like figures adorn the top and sides.

But it is the harmonious music of the Bell Wagon that has made this vehicle a legend. The chiming resonance that fills the air for miles is simply too unique to put into words.

I became enraptured by this wagon—the effect it has had on its audience, the design and craftsmanship that went into its building, its place in the circus over the decades—and began researching it. Then, in the 1950s, I was fortunate enough to meet one of the men that helped create the Bell Wagon, Henry Moeller Jr.

The small town of Baraboo, Wisconsin is rich with circus history, but never so much as when this man was alive. When I met Henry, I was immediately fascinated by his style. He liked things the "old way" and made no

THREE COMPANIES combined efforts to build the Bell Wagon. The Centennial Bell Foundry (above) casted the bells, The Milwaukee Ornamental Wood Carving Co. crafted the wood carvings, and Moeller Wagon Works (below) built the wagon itself and put everything together.

THE BELL WAGON after a recent trip through the restoration shop. One of the most talked about wagons in circus history, it is beautiful to behold and even more so to hear.

attempt to hide it. Henry still spent his time in an office located in the corner of his old shop, Moeller Wagon Works—the rest of the building he leased to an auto dealer.

Folks would crowd into this warm little office, as Henry "held court" every day around lunchtime. The walls, peppered with old circus posters and photographs, set the tone. We'd gather 'round with a cup of coffee or a plug of tobacco and listen to Henry spin his tales. Soon, the talk would turn to the circus and we'd find ourselves drifting back in time, to the 1890s.

Outside the window, paved streets turned to dirt and the sound of evening traffic reminded us of the gentle clip-clop of shod horses. Noises from the car dealership brought the wagon shop to life—hot anvils being pounded...the determined craftsman hard at work. And just up the street, as we all knew, stood an old brick house—the home of seven young brothers known as the Ringlings.

The Ringlings, of course, went on to stage America's most famous circus. And it all began in Baraboo, in 1884. Henry Moeller, his father, Henry Sr., and his brother, Corwin, helped put the Ringlings on wheels.

"For the first 6 years the Ringling Circus was on the road, they moved from town to town by horse-drawn

---

"The Ringlings reached the point where they really needed a showstopper—something that would put them at the top of the heap. This is where the Bell Wagon came in..."

---

wagons." Henry once told me. "We built dozens and dozens of these wagons for the Ringlings...and lots of other circuses too, like the Gollmars and the Sparks. But the Ringlings were special. They were true showmen.

"Whenever the Ringlings wanted a wagon, all we had to know were the basic dimensions, the length and what kind of a load it would carry. Did they want the top opened or closed...racks on the side or not? Once I had this information, I'd make a pencil drawing with the dimensions on it and take it to one of the brothers. When the plans were okayed, we'd build the wagon!

"Then, in 1890, the Ringlings changed their circus to a railroad show, moving on a total of 18 cars," Henry said. "Thinking they were headed for the big time, they purchased a bunch of wagons and equipment from the Adam Forepaugh Show. And they were right—1890 and 1891 *were* very good to them.

"So the Ringlings had reached the point where they really wanted to expand. They needed a showstopper—something that would put them at the top of the heap. This is where the Bell Wagon came in. I think it was the first major parade wagon they ever dreamed up and purchased as new.

"We (Moeller Wagon Works) were assigned the task of crafting that dream into a reality, and it was one of the most rewarding challenges of my life."

Music in the Streets

Circuses traditionally carried a variety of musical units for their parades. In addition to the bands that sat on top of wagons, they used band organs, una-fones, chimes, air and steam calliopes and many tinkling bells.

But the Ringlings did not want bells that tinkled. They wanted the bong variety. And that's what they got.

The Centennial Bell Foundry in

Milwaukee provided nine gigantic bronze bells that, combined, weigh 4,300 lbs. They range in diameter at the base from 20-1/4 to 35-5/16 inches. At the foundry, the bells were cast and fitted with clappers. Then they were mounted onto a massive oak frame.

This structure was shipped to the Moeller Wagon Works in February 1892, according to Henry, where it was all fitted onto an undercarriage built by the Moellers.

Next, they flashed up the wagon in true circus fashion. This was done with stunning wood carvings made by the artists at the Milwaukee Ornamental Wood Carving Co. When the wood carvings arrived in Baraboo, the Moellers worked to fasten the pieces onto the framework.

The finished product is what many consider to be the most remarkable circus parade wagon in existence. Three other "chime" wagons were built in the 19th century, but this one was by far the standout, and happens to be the only survivor.

Sounding the Bells

The bell ringer sits at the back of the wagon facing the nine spring-primed levers. Pulling these levers that are connected to the clappers by wires rings the bells. Each bell, of course, carries a different pitch and tonal characteristic.

ILLUSTRATIONS advertising the Bell Wagon brought crowds in throngs to see and hear it…and helped push the Ringling Bros. to the top of the circus world.

Circus historians tell us that Al Ringling favored church tunes on the bells. Some songs played by the carillonneur included *My Old Kentucky Home*, *Dixie*, *Greenland's Icy Mountains*, *Rock of Ages* and many others.

The Ringlings assigned Robert Meek to drive the eight bay Percherons that pulled the wagon, and in 1892 this fabulous wagon was unveiled.

The press agents for the Ringling Circus couldn't restrain their enthusiasm. Not only did they indicate that the bells came from Russia, but they also proclaimed: "Continuous Carillons or Tremendous Tones from Tons and Tons of Sweet-Toned Bells. Or, the Largest, Grandest, Heaviest Chimes Ever Heard in America."

And they weren't through.

"These mighty Russian chimes," they continued, "fill the air for miles with broken but melodious whispers like the tremendous tones of the music of many waters."

On April 30, 1892 the people of Baraboo were the first in the world to witness the historic Bell Wagon. And according to Henry Moeller, they were not disappointed. "Word got around long before the wagon was completed, that something was brewing in our wagon shop. When we finally finished, folks just couldn't get enough of hearing those bells ring!"

THE PLAYER of the nine chromatically arranged bells, or the carillonneur, sits at the rear end of the wagon, and faces the nine spring-primed levers that are connected by cables to the clappers. As the levers are pulled, 4,300 lbs. of bells "fill the air for miles like the tremendous tones of the music of many waters". These revealing photographs, taken in 1949, highlight some of the hand-carved figures of the era.

CHARLIE TALWORTH was the driver of the eight bay Percherons in this 1895 photograph.

Then the circus hit the road, staging parades and putting up their tents in such places as Anamosa, Iowa; York, Nebraska; and Bowling Green, Ohio. They also played some larger cities like Milwaukee, Omaha, Kansas City and Oklahoma City.

And so the Ringling Bros. Circus grew and grew, and the Bell Wagon remained a parade highlight for nearly 20 years before it was put into storage in the 1920s, when the Ringlings discontinued their street parades.

Today, some Baraboo businessmen fondly recall the days when they were kids back in the 1920s. It was sort of a neighborhood ritual to sneak into the Ringling barns and whack the big bells with a two-by-four.

The Ringlings loaned the Bell Wagon to the Hagenbeck-Wallace Circus (which they also owned) in 1934. After that season, it went into storage until

---

"Although some of the wood was replaced, most of the Bell Wagon remains intact today…"

1941. For the next decade, off and on, it toured with Ringling Bros. and Barnum & Bailey Circus.

In this time, the Bell Wagon did not appear in street parades, but in a variety of publicity spectacles the circus staged each year. As always, it was pulled by six beautifully matched Percherons.

Then the wagon was put into storage once again, this time until 1984. Kenneth Feld, president of Ringling Bros. and Barnum & Bailey Combined Shows, decided to loan the wagon to the Circus World Museum so it could take part in the Great Circus Parade.

With that, the wagon restoration shop came to life in a real hurry. Marv Gauger, the museum's original wagon master, came out of retirement to oversee the operation. Museum records estimate Marv and his crew put in over 1,100 hours of work to make this aged beauty street-worthy.

When I see the Bell Wagon on parade these days, l ask myself: What would wonderful old Henry Moeller say if he were still around and holding daily court in his office? Perhaps he

WITH THE DISCONTINUATION of their street parade, the Ringlings retired the Bell Wagon in 1920. In 1941, it was taken out of storage and used in the circus for another decade or so (below, 1949). The wagon then remained in storage until 1984, when the Ringling Bros. loaned it to the Circus World Museum.

Ron Brayer

Ron Brayer

THE BELL WAGON arrived at the Circus World Museum's restoration shop in 1984. Above, the original frame of the wagon shows the curse of 93 years—dry rot necessitated replacing all of the major beams. The entire wagon had to be completely disassembled—bells wood carvings, undercarriage and all. And although some wood had to be replaced, most of the original Bell Wagon remains intact today.

would stomp his foot and complain that we weren't taking good enough care of his pride and joy.

Maybe he would gaze at the wagon and recall some old story—a problem the Moellers had with a wagon, or one of the Ringlings getting into a jam of some sort. Or he would tell of that day the Bell Wagon was finished in 1892,

and he and his crew posed proudly for a photograph in the Wisconsin sun.

My own guess is that Henry would have hit the ceiling, because the circus put pneumatic tires on the undercarriage in the 1940s. I can just see him spitting a stream of tobacco juice into the 5-gallon paint bucket he used as an office spittoon. "What have you

done with the St. Mary's Wheels?" he would bark.

But in the end, Henry would be overjoyed that although this wagon has changed a little—an updated set of wheels, a new coat of paint…some replaced wood—the magic and the legend of the Bell Wagon continues to live on.

Ron Brayer

RESTORATION proceeds under the expert guidance of Marv Gauger (in checked shirt) and Harold Burdick. Marv headed the restoration shop for many years, and then came out of retirement to restore the Bell Wagon on a volunteer basis. Museum records indicate Marv and his crew put in over 1,100 hours to make the Bell Wagon street-worthy.

FREDERICK EGGERT was one of the artists that worked at the Milwaukee Ornamental Wood Carving Co.

TIM PERKINS carefully removes scores of layers of paint from th
wood carvings.

FILM PRODUCER Cecil B. De Mille (on right in photo at left) visi
with Henry Moeller (center) and Henry's cousin Henry Ringlir
North during filming of *The Greatest Show on Earth* in 1951. It we
on to win Best Picture that year. Below: The Bell Wagon rides in th
Great Circus Parade in 1992—100 years after its creation!

Folk Art On Parade

The great circus street parades of years gone by were sort of like an animated museum exhibit. Some of the finest examples of hand-crafted artistry of the period rolled through American and European towns and cities in the form of glorious wood carvings displayed on the sides of circus wagons.

es. Imaginary creatures, gargoyles and griffins were worked into the designs. Biblical characters, Roman gladiators and soldiers looked out from the sides or corners of cages and tableaux.

Legendary figures such as Columbus and John Bull adorned some wagons, while fictional characters ranging from Robinson Crusoe and Sinbad to Cinderella and Santa Claus were depicted

Great Circus Parade Inc.

In the hey-day of the circus parades, wood carvings could be found all over town. Advertising signs hung along the streets were made of wood: A huge tooth might be used to identify a dentist's office; or there might be an Indian outside the tobacco store.

There were so many wood carvings around town that people took this beauty for granted. But today, these items are of great value. A merry-go-round horse built in 1900 will frequently bring $10,000 at an antique auction. Likewise, a circus wagon built in that period for $1,500 would be appraised today for $100,000 or more.

But why do we call the wagons folk art? Because the carvings were not simply a means to catch the eye—the artwork represents the many different aspects of our civilization. The customs, arts, crafts, legends and superstitions of 19th-century man are etched into the sides of these wagons.

These artists of wood did a stunning job. Great leafy scrolls and swirls surrounded Greek goddess-

THE WOOD-CARVERS produced head studies of the people of the Americas. The other side of the America Steam Calliope depicts six additional races.

A BEAUTIFUL FIGURINE (below) from the Great Britain Bandwagon.

Jim Morrill

on others. Cupids were another favorite subject of the wood-carvers.

Ferocious animals, typically lions, either in mortal combat or posing majestically, were frequently portrayed. And other animals, like elephants, birds and even a kangaroo, could find their way onto a wagon's side. The large wagons were often decorated with mirrors or featured colorful landscape paintings.

The planned visual effect of a parade wagon went right down to the color of the horses pulling it. A white wagon with silver carvings would likely be pulled by six or eight coal-black horses with white feather plumes in their bridles. Cage wagons were usually painted orange, green or red with gold or silver trim to highlight the appearance of their wild cargo.

In any case, the appearance of a wagon was always intended to create an emotional response…it had to stir the parade audience up a little. And since no two wagons were ever alike, a mile-long procession of wagons meant an awful lot of ooh's and aah's.

But before the wood-carvers started working, the wagon had to be built, and it is important to note that wagon building and wood

THE BANDWAGON from Pawnee Bill's show is one of the greatest examples of folk art in existence. Several scenarios portray the spirit of early America with vivid detail. Columbus discovering America (below) is on one side, while the other side depicts Pocahontas saving Captain John Smith from execution. Above those are carvings of an Indian, Pawnee Bill and the mighty buffalo.

carving were two separate crafts altogether.

The circus would start the whole process off by contacting a wagon company and giving the orders for the style, size and heft of the vehicle they wanted. It was up to the wagon builder to design the wagon and send back the sketch for an approval.

Some wagon companies specialized, and would build only circus wagons, for example. Others would produce whatever a company wanted—beer wagons, milk wagons or dump wagons.

Moeller Bros. Wagon Works of Baraboo built a great many circus wagons for the Ringling Bros. and others. The

Bode Wagon Works of Cincinnati built the Snake Den and Great Britain Bandwagon that are in the Circus World Museum collection. The Sebastian Wagon Works of New York City constructed particularly elegant wagons like the America and Asia Tableaux and the Golden Age of Chivalry, which are still with us today.

Although these wagons often appeared to be very luxurious, durable

construction was always the first priority. Circus wagons were subject to some very rough treatment during the show season. Before the railroads, remember, these wagons carried the entire show

AT ONE TIME, wood-carved art was commonplace in America. A wooden Indian like the one at right used to signify the tobacco store. Today, these items are considered folk art and are highly sought after.

AN ANTIQUE MERRY-GO-ROUND HORSE (above) will often bring $10,000 at an auction.

A HANDSOME FIGURE from the corner of the Barnum & Bailey and Hutchinson Cage Wagon (left; also see page 87).

from town to town—for months on end.

But they also had to be attractive for the audience, and this is where the wood-carvers came in to play. Some wagon builders had so much business that they could support their own wood carving department. Most, however, preferred to have their carvings made by ornamental wood carving specialists.

The wood carvings on these circus wagons were usually created by the crafted artisans who immigrated to America from Europe, and brought with them age-old sculpting traditions.

It was up to the circus owners to come up with the different themes they wanted in their parade. They would inspire the wood-carvers with ideas and request the type and size of carvings they would like.

For example, in 1903, the Ringling Bros. decided they wanted a wagon that would pay tribute to Great Britain. The

THIS SIDE of the Two Hemispheres Bandwagon features the eastern hemisphere of the earth and pays tribute to some of the countries of that region with their shield and flag. The western hemisphere appears on the left side. Below, a close-up view of the emblem from the France Bandwagon.

artists would go to work and come up with John Bull, the Queen or a royal crest. These carvings were in turn

> *"The customs, arts, crafts, legends and superstitions of 19th-century man are etched into the sides of these wagons..."*

passed on to the wagon builders, who would fasten them to the wagons and paint the entire vehicle.

In the old parade days, the carvings were usually coated with gold leaf, or occasionally silver leaf, to decorate the wood. When the wagons weren't on

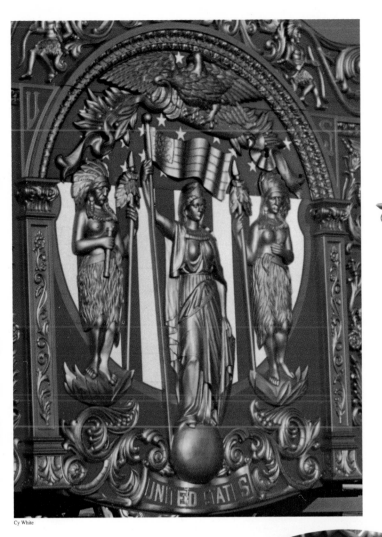

Cy White

Jim Morrill

SEVERAL WAGONS in the museum's collection were built to honor a particular country. Above is the United States Bandwagon.

THE COLUMBIA BANDWAGON (above). The Great Britain Bandwagon (left) features John Bull.

parade, the figures were covered with canvas, lined with soft felt, to shield them from the rain and sun.

New Ideas

In 1919, as a new venture, the Bode firm built a series of wagons for the U.S. Motorized Circus. Standard wagon bodies, each representing a different country, were built and then mounted onto truck chassis. Carved on their sides were flags, emblems and coats of arms of the nations involved.

GREAT BRITAIN

Unfortunately, deplorable road conditions brought this circus venture to its knees. When the truck show failed, the bodies were installed on horse-drawn wagon undercarriages and paraded for years.

The France Bandwagon is the only vehicle of this wonderful group that is extant—and it rolls down Milwaukee streets in the Great Circus Parade.

In the 1880s the Barnum & Bailey Circus built a series of

J&J Images

J&J Images

THE SWAN BANDWAGON is decorated with mythical maidens, children and fanciful creatures of the sea. Even under close inspection, exquisite detail of the 1905 woodwork is stunning.

J&J Images

pony-drawn floats, each with allegorical carvings representing nursery rhymes. These seven enchanting floats were used in the "Children's Section" of the street parade. Three of these charming vehicles still exist and are in the collection at the Circus World Museum:

Mother Goose, Cinderella and the Old Woman in the Shoe (see Chapter 6).

The Circus World Museum cherishes every wagon in its collection, which is the largest in the world. Valued at almost $5 million, these historic masterpieces are irreplaceable.

But their monetary value is not what's important. The fact that they still exist for all of us to appreciate, is, as they are a constant reminder of a time when although technology was primitive, man's yearning for beauty and mastery of art was not.

TABLEAU WAGONS, like the Kangaroo Tableau (upper left), were often painted with colorful murals or landscapes.

THE ELEPHANT TABLEAU (top) pays homage to the circus' favorite animal.

THE STORK (left) delivering a child—another myth—is found on a Hagenbeck-Wallace Bandwagon.

THE SUBTLE CARVINGS of the Beauty Tableau (above) are appropriate to this wagon's title.

THE NOBLE LION has been a favorite subject for wood-carvers around the world for centuries. Since many lions appear in the circus, wagons presented an excellent opportunity to display these majestic beasts either in action or posing. Lions are also featured in the two wagons at far right from the Hagenbeck-Wallace Circus of the 1920s.

A ROMAN SOLDIER (above) appears on the Gladiator Tableau.

GREAT ATTENTION TO DETAIL was carried out, right down to the wheels of the wagons. Most frequently, wheels were painted red in the center, blending into orange, then yellow. This design became known as "sunburst wheels" because as they revolved, people imagined they were seeing the rays of a setting sun. Longer spokes (right), wooden plates (above) and a wider variety of colors were used to make the wagon procession even more eye-catching.

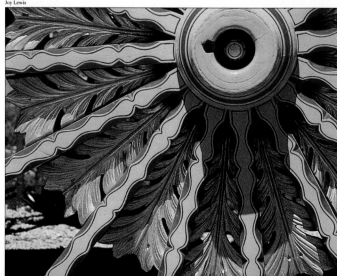

Looking Back at The Golden Years of America's Circus Parades

CHAPTER NINE

The circus street parades that began to flourish in the mid-1800s were actually conceived of as a form of advertising. In other words, the parade was simply a way to let people know that the circus had come to town.

A traveling circus, with all of its equipment, animals and performers, represented an enormous financial investment. Show owners couldn't afford a small crowd turnout, so they did whatever they could to lure the townsfolk into the big top. The great lengths to which they went to publicize their shows were years ahead of their time.

At least 2 weeks before circus day, the advertising brigades from the show began pasting the walls of barns, sheds and fences with exciting lithographs. These posters, printed in many brilliant colors, were illustrated with graceful bareback riders on white horses, charging tigers, clowns and acrobats of all descriptions.

Hundreds more lithographs were hung in the windows of almost every store in town, proclaiming the date and time of the upcoming circus performance. In addition, circuses mailed circulars by the thousands to everyone on the mail routes.

Newspaper advertisements, often filling full pages, declared in huge letters, "Coming Soon, Coming Sure" or "Wait for the Big One", which further contributed to the suspense of the upcoming spectacle.

As these messages saturated the population, they stirred conversations and whetted appetites. It would have been nearly impossible to have missed the news that the circus was coming...but just in case, the showmen saved their very best effort for last—the free, horse-drawn circus street parade!

Started Small

In the late 18th century, circus troupes were made up mostly of equestrians who put on colorful wardrobe and marched through the streets.

By 1825 circuses began using tents, so wagons were needed to haul the equipment. They also needed cages and dens to carry the wild animals.

As the show grew in size, more wagons and

A CAPITAL CIRCUS. Hagenbeck-Wallace Circus parades down the streets of Washington, D.C. around 1930.

THE JOHN ROBINSON CIRCUS wending its way through a maze of people in 1900. Mirror tableau wagon shows the reflection of its admirers.

A MAJESTICALLY outfitted elephant with passengers lumbering down main street in the Sells Floto Circus Parade, 1924.

ONE OF THE MOST unusual parade units was the 16-camel hitch that appeared in the Ringling Bros. Circus Parade (below). This photo and the one at lower right were taken in Lewiston, Maine in 1911.

horses were added, and the acquisition of elephants and camels improved the circus and certainly the parade.

Soon, all of the competing circuses caught on to the idea, and the free procession through town became an expected prelude to the circus performance. From the caged animals, elephants, horses, performers and clowns, to the beautiful wagons, floats and unusual mechanical instruments, the street parade aroused people and brought them to the show grounds.

In the street, the size, quality and diversity of a particular circus were under the scrutiny of its audience. The number of elephants and wagons or the quality of stock and menagerie were

---

"Circus parades reached their zenith between 1880 and 1920..."

---

usually good indicators of the caliber of the circus performance.

The circus parade was expected to measure up to or exceed the claims of its advertisements. If it did not, people would be less likely to pay for the show.

This unique and dazzling spectacle was enough to overwhelm any audi-

ence. It played on the three key senses of man. Obvious were the colorful sights of the wardrobe and the ornate tableau wagons. And the rousing music of the mounted bands, calliopes, una-fones and band organs lent a celebratory air to the march.

But there were also the smells! They were never mentioned, yet they were

there—strong, acrid, and exotic. Hundreds of sweating horses...strange scents from wild animals from foreign lands seeping from cages and dens... and the unusual smell of 20 camels or 40 elephants shuffling by...they just can't be described.

Crowds Followed Calliope

Resistance melted, willpower ebbed

BY 1939, all of the big circuses had discontinued their parades, but the lure was still there. Crowds were always on hand to watch the action at the railroad yards.

to a minimum, and as the last notes of the calliope echoed down the street, thousands found themselves following its trail of white smoke. Even those who had expressed a borderline interest decided that they just might have to attend after all.

When they trekked to the show grounds in throngs and bought tickets to the show, the parade had served its purpose.

The circus parade reached its zenith in the period of about 1880-1920, when its elegance and length increased dramatically from year to year.

Showmen spent freely to improve their circus, buying more exotic animals and glorious tableau wagons…and constantly enlarging their army of performers, equestrians, clowns and musicians.

In fact, circus parades were so successful that they began competing with the shows they were intended to advertise. The free parade was entertaining enough, and some families decided against attending the circus itself, which cost money.

Early in the century, Barnum & Bailey tried to discontinue the parade, but were forced to restore it by popular demand. In 1920, however, the great combine, Ringling Bros. and Barnum & Bailey Circus, discontinued its street parade.

One by one, other circuses followed suit. Al G. Barnes, a circus owner, complained bitterly that traffic signals broke his parade into segments, completely spoiling the effect. The Cole Bros. Circus parade of 1939 was the last that can be remotely compared to the marches of the turn of the century.

There were several reasons for the demise of circus parades. Cities could not afford to have traffic tied up by a slow-moving horse-drawn pageant. The heavy wagons cut up asphalt paving in hot weather. Charles Ringling said performers of daring feats could not give their best after a long, hot, dusty ride through the streets.

Perhaps the foremost reason for dis-

continuing parades was that, generally speaking, urban sprawl pushed the show grounds farther and farther away from the center of the city. This often meant a 5- to 10-mile haul just to get downtown. Then they had to go back to the show grounds and prepare for two circus performances—there just wasn't enough time.

So the circus parade succumbed to progress. Trucks and tractors replaced the great draft horses and wagons and eventually, the railroad, too. Luckily, folks can still witness the magic of the circus under the big top—today more than 40 circuses in America are still going strong.

The unique and glorious page of American history known as the circus street parade has been turned, but not forgotten. Books, photographs and memories keep it alive. And a magnificent reenactment, staged every year in Milwaukee brings it to within arm's reach of thousands of people.

1911 Parade Review

The Hagenbeck-Wallace street parade at Peru, Indiana on April 20, 1911 was reviewed in the April 29 issue of *Billboard* magazine.

This review gives us an indication of how people viewed a circus parade at the turn of the century. Everything from the quality of the horses to the color of the wardrobe was appreciated.

"There probably never was a more brilliant, well-planned and better laid-

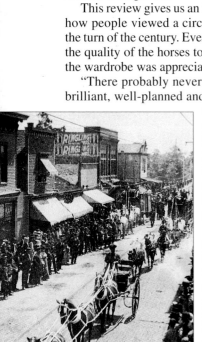

out circus parade than that which took its way through the streets of Peru, Indiana April 20.

"One novelty, the first in order of the many noted in this particular pageant, was a brilliant cortege of lady couriers, riding on gaily caparisoned horses before the big bandwagon.

"The horses, not less than the riders, seemed imbued with the spirit of the occasion. They pranced along playfully, stepping proudly and switching their beribboned tails in friendly greeting to the enthusiastic spectators.

CIRCUS DAY was like a holiday...stores closed, chores were put on hold and everybody was in good spirits. Left, a random hitch in 1903. Below, the Barnum & Bailey Circus parade in Long Branch, New Jersey, 1912.

BLACK RIVER FALLS, Wisconsin welcomed the Ringling Bros. Circus on August 17, 1892. The huge billing stand across the intersection is also advertising the cir-

and measure proverbial.

"Four brilliant tandems followed the bandwagon. The horses were the choice of the Wallace ring stock, and the riders were the prettiest of the equestriennes. Their wardrobe consisted of brilliant riding habits of pink, gold, old rose and green, thickly spangled with silver.

"Their approach was greeted with vociferous cheers, which they acknowledged with graceful nods that sent their long plumes into sparkling undulations in the sunshine. Each rider had her particular admirers, and there was some competition as to which class of followers could show their appreciation loudest.

"Following the tandems came one tableau wagon, drawn by eight horses; open dens of tigers and lions, drawn by

" 'Just watch me,' some of the young horses appeared to say. This seemed to create a rivalry among the older horses, those which had marched in parades before, and they lifted up their heads and stepped as lightly and with as much spirit as their younger colleagues.

"The Wallace show has always been noted for the beauty of its stock. Its reputation was never based on better grounds than those which characterize it this year. The horses are well fed, well groomed and of the best mettle obtainable.

"Professor Merric directed his band with vim and gusto. He is proud of his aggregation of musicians. He wanted

THE DAYS OF BIG ZOOS had not yet arrived, so displays like this one were very educational.

them to show what they could do, and they, being no less anxious than he, ripped out their music in volume

six horses; tableau, by six colts; open den with hippopotamus, eight horses; then a company of beautifully costumed ladies, on brilliantly caparisoned stock from the Wallace stables.

"Then followed an open den of llamas, drawn by six horses; a clown riding a donkey cart; two four-horse tableaux; a clown riding a donkey; four-horse tableau; six-horse tableau; clown driving a donkey; open den of axis deer, four horses; open den elks and kangaroos, six horses; open den snake enchantress, six horses; clown bandwagon, drawn by six horses; another company of 10 lady riders; and two Roman chariots.

"Four hybrids (cross between a zebra and mule; novelty); tableau, four horses; Oriental mounted band; open

DAPPLE GRAY Percherons in the Cole Bros. Circus making their way to the show grounds in 1939.

den of lions, eight horses; four-horse tableau; sideshow bandwagon, eight horses; 12 mounted men garbed in brilliant military uniforms; juvenile Roman Hippodrome (each driving miniature chariots, drawn by ponies).

"Finally, 10 thoroughbred ponies; four-horse tableau; Russian ladies and men (a feature with the show as singers and dancers), eight horses; six-horse tableau, or closed den; four-horse open den, elk (see his antlers!); six-horse tableau; 13 elephants; four camels; and a calliope drawn by six horses."

BEAUTIFULLY OUTFITTED equestriennes were a favorite of every circus parade—these ladies are riding sidesaddle.

THE 1901 RINGLING BROS. CIRCUS featured this troupe of girls riding white horses sidesaddle. Their dresses are red velvet, trimmed with gold braid.

THE 40-HORSE HITCH in Brooklyn, New York in 1904 (below). Jake Posey was the man behind the reins. This incredible feat of horsemanship was not repeated until 1972.

FEW CIRCUSES were big enough to stage a 40-horse hitch. In 1903, Barnum & Bailey wanted people to know that their show was truly a whopper. The circus boasted that the 40 Percherons, along with the Two-Hemispheres Bandwagon, was a $50,000 investment.

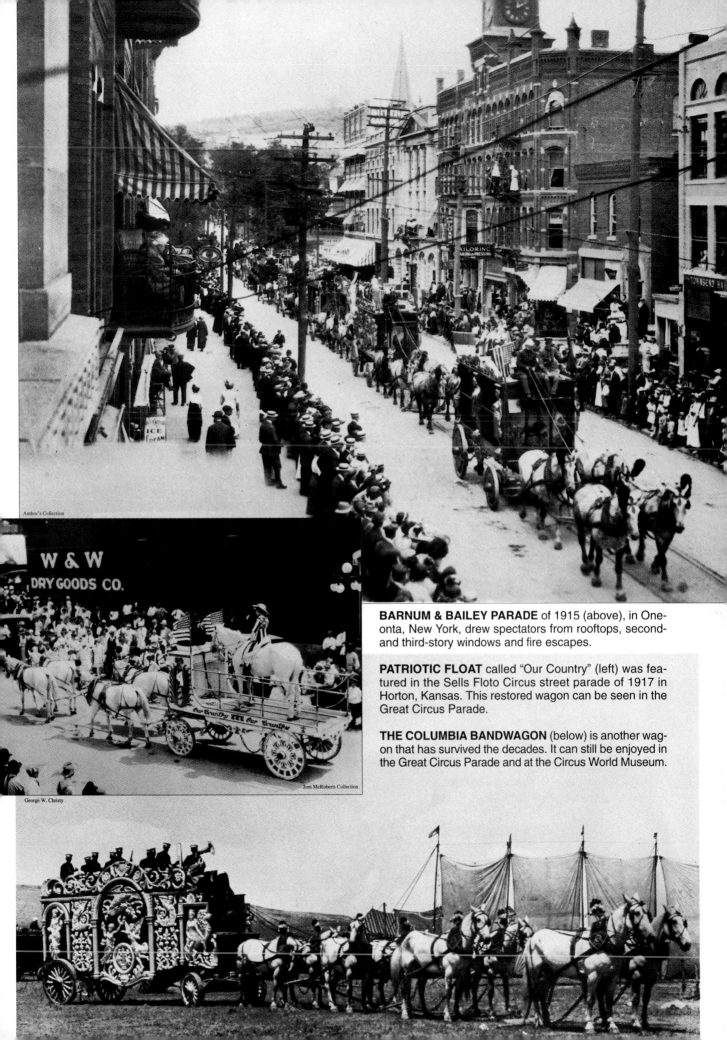

BARNUM & BAILEY PARADE of 1915 (above), in Oneonta, New York, drew spectators from rooftops, second- and third-story windows and fire escapes.

PATRIOTIC FLOAT called "Our Country" (left) was featured in the Sells Floto Circus street parade of 1917 in Horton, Kansas. This restored wagon can be seen in the Great Circus Parade.

THE COLUMBIA BANDWAGON (below) is another wagon that has survived the decades. It can still be enjoyed in the Great Circus Parade and at the Circus World Museum.

END OF AN ERA. Photo above is the Cole Bros. final street parade in 1939. Most circuses had given up parades several years prior to that.

YOUNG BOYS could always be found around the clown carts (right). Below, an eight-horse hitch of Percherons leans into their collars at the Milwaukee lakefront show grounds in 1935.

How the Show Grounds Bring the Circus to Life

When the Great Circus Parade started out in 1963, we realized that we needed an assembly area—a place to headquarter the parade, gather the troupes and hitch the horses to the wagons. For the first 2 years we somehow managed to do this from the lower end of a narrow street (North Jefferson) adjacent to a vacant lot.

Well, if this cramped area wasn't enough to prompt a change, the feeling that there was enough fun and excitement going on to share with the public, was. We just needed a wide-open space to display our wares, and a whole new dimension could open up for the parade.

Milwaukee County was pleased to provide the Circus World Museum with Veterans Park. Right on the breezy shores of Lake Michigan, covered with acres and acres of lush green grass, this park, for 3 days in July, becomes what we now refer to as the show grounds.

The show grounds still serve their original purpose as the "setup area" for the parade, but over the years more features have been added, and more and more people show up to take a "behind

"CIRCUS IN THE SKY" shakes the foundations of downtown Milwaukee and lights up the show grounds every year on the night before the Great Circus Parade.

the scenes" look into the Great Circus Parade.

Quite simply, the show grounds are a gigantic world of organized circus mayhem—one of the most unique and fabulously fun weekend events in America. Folks find themselves showered with all of the attractions of the circus, past *and* present—not just to look at—but to reach out and touch, hear, smell and taste!

Like the Great Circus Parade, admission to the show grounds is free. There is, however, a charge for those who wish to attend the famed Hanneford Circus performance, featured beneath an old-fashioned big top three times daily.

Stroll Through the Grounds

The enormous collection of 70 or so beautiful parade wagons is displayed throughout the park for people to admire at their leisure. These precious wagons seem to roll by so fast in the parade, some folks like the opportunity

"FORMAL PORTRAIT". Wagons are lined up for a photograph in 1964 (above). The wagon collection has since tripled. Below left: Watching each of the drivers make a practice run around the grounds has been a crowd favorite for years. The spacious Veterans Park, along the shores of Lake Michigan (below right), is an ideal location for the 3-day circus extravaganza.

ENTERTAINING AND EDUCATIONAL. The Circus World Museum sets up an enormous collection of exhibits, displays, artwork and other interesting historical memorabilia on the show grounds.

to give them a real up-close inspection.

Then there are the horses...hundreds of powerful draft horses and riding horses. A feeling of suspense and excitement is in the air, as everyone knows the parade is just around the corner, including the horses. Watching the big hitches make a couple of "practice runs" around the park with their parade wagon has become a crowd favorite.

Peanuts, popcorn, snow cones, cotton candy, sandwiches...a gold mine of snack foods entice hungry passersby with their mouth-watering aromas. For a true "taste of the circus", the show grounds are hard to beat.

The rousing and rambunctious melodies of many circus instruments spread a cheerful atmosphere all over the park. Regular concerts are scheduled on the Steam Calliope and the Bell Wagon.

Three or four antique band organs are strategically located on the grounds,

so there is festive circus music in the air.

Children enjoy the petting zoo, camel rides, elephant rides, the menagerie of wild animals and, of course, the parade horse tents. Here, the circus parade reveals itself to visitors in a living,

---

"The 70 or so beautiful parade wagons are displayed throughout the park for people to admire at their leisure..."

---

breathing form—and kids especially cherish the experience.

Another area has a tent where children can get their faces painted like a clown. Still another tent offers a special clown show.

It seems every time you turn around, there is something new to see or do.

And there are free circus acts, outside the big top, for everyone to enjoy. In 1992, a daring man performed on a trapeze that hung below a helicopter. There have been daredevils shot out of a cannon, and high-wire acts that draw the attention of thousands to the sky.

The Horse Fair, featuring 70 horses, ponies, mules and donkeys, is a fascinating addition to the show grounds. It has proved both educational and entertaining. Today, children and also many adults do not have the opportunity to see various horse breeds or learn anything about them. At the Horse Fair, several breeds are represented, and the men who raise and own these horses are on hand to answer questions and explain the outstanding features of their horses.

Once, while visiting the Horse Fair tent, I heard a rather well-dressed woman with three kids in tow point to a mule and ask one of the attendants, "Are these horses or cows?" When you

stop to think about it, there aren't many places for city people to see horses today. Not at the zoo; not on the city streets; *maybe* at the state fair.

Since the Circus Parade is indebted to the horse—with all the horse-drawn wagons and scores of riding horses—we feel obligated to make the effort to educate people. When they understand what they are seeing, it makes the whole parade week more meaningful.

Also at the show grounds, the Circus World Museum is trying out the idea of an exhibit on circus history—just a taste of what a family would see if they came to the museum in Baraboo. The staff wants visitors to get a feel for the rich history of the circus in America. There are the many beautiful wood-carved wagons, original circus posters,

THE HORSE TENTS, featuring some of the 750 horses appearing in the Great Circus Parade, are an incredible sight (above). At the Horse Fair (left and top), many breeds of horses, ponies, mules and donkeys can be seen, and owners are on hand to answer questions and educate the public.

FRIENDLY FALLOW DEER at the petting zoo are waiting to make some new friends.

wardrobe and educational displays.

Parade Draws Near

Curious visitors also have the opportunity to peer into the Wardrobe Tent and feast their eyes on the vast collection of glittering clothing, as the department prepares to outfit the parade's nearly 1,000 participants.

Also on hand is the "Wagon Shop", headed by Harold Burdick, the Circus World Museum's Superintendent of Wagons. He and his crew use wagon #53 as their headquarters. Fully equipped with an array of tools, this crew is ready to repair any last-minute wagon problems that pop up. Groups of onlookers always find this an interesting craft to behold.

Finally, as parade time draws near on Sunday morning, the show grounds sparkle with anticipation. Parade participants and volunteer help are hustling now, making last-minute adjustments, getting into period costumes and securing their position.

The occasional notes of a trumpet, tuba or bass drum signal that the bands are warming up and getting into formation.

The horses are all groomed, looking

UNUSUAL ENTERTAINMENT—such as camel and elephant rides (a family favorite)—is offered at the show grounds.

HUGE BOA CONSTRICTORS ride with the Humbert girls in the glass-sided Ringling Snake Den during the parade.

CROWDS OF CHILDREN sketch their favorite wagon, visit the exhibit tents or just soak up the excitement.

proud, anxious and noble in their polished harness and feather plumes. Soon, the drivers start hitching their teams to the wagons, and the gentle knock of the turning wheels heading for the reviewing stand tells us that the Great Circus Parade is ready to roll.

MICHELANGELO'S TRAPEZE ACT from a helicopter drew the attention of thousands to the air in 1992.

TWO TROUPERS. Lou Jacobs (left) was a Ringling Bros. clown for 50 years, and Dr. J.Y. Henerson was a veterinarian with Ringling for 35 years.

FAMILY AFFAIR. Three Strongs (from left), Matt and his parents, Donna and Dick, participated in the 1988 parade.

CHILDREN LOVE to have their faces painted like a clown or find themselves the center of amusement in the Hospital Clown Show (below).

The Excitement Builds...
Prelude to the Parade

CHAPTER ELEVEN

The majority of the estimated 750,000 people that line the Milwaukee streets to view the Great Circus Parade arrive early Sunday morning to ensure a good viewing position. Hundreds of others, however, start staking their claim as early as Friday and Saturday.

These families really make a weekend out of the parade. They bring tents, coolers, cooking equipment, even TV's and radios—all the luxuries of home—as they wait patiently and leisurely for the big event. They play cards, barbecue, visit the show grounds and, of course, look forward to Sunday afternoon. I don't know what's more fun for them, the camping out or the parade, but nobody's complaining— it's all in the name of fun.

When planning the very first Great Circus Parade, it occurred to us that maybe we could stage a prelude to sort of kick things off. It

would cut down a little on the waiting and kind of "warm up" the audience for the big parade.

What's more, with a prelude parade, we could get even more members of the community in on the volunteer action. And we would have the opportunity to

explore yet another historical venue.

The Prelude Parade, like the Circus Train, show grounds and Great Circus Parade, is based on a historical American tradition. It used to be customary for small towns to stage parades on the Fourth of July (or other occasions), and anything that moved could enter.

Folks would join the procession on bicycles, horses, automobiles or maybe just an old truck. The police, fire and transit departments always got in on the act, too. These parades were a great opportunity for the whole community to get together and have fun.

The Prelude Parade is staged in the spirit of those old community processions. There are some very fine restored classic vehicles, nearly 40 antique cars, high-wheel bicycles (also known as penny-farthings), old fire engines, motorized trolley cars, dignitaries riding in carriages, a mounted police patrol, a color guard and much more.

Seeing these old-time vehicles parade gaily down the packed streets is truly a unique experience. For a

Frankie B. Cole

Frankie B. Cole

PROCESSION OF PENNY-FAR-THINGS from the 1890s (left) is a favorite attraction of the Prelude Parade. Above, classic autos roll down Wisconsin Avenue.

STAKING OUT a good viewing spot along the 4-mile parade route has become a ritual for some people. Many arrive as early as Friday or Saturday for the parade that always starts at 2 p.m. Sunday. Thousands line chairs along the streets, but others have much more elaborate setups with tents and cooking equipment (below left). Below right: A parking garage provides good "box seats" for spectators.

moment, it's easy to get lost and forget what year it is…the automobiles sparkle like brand new, fire engines clang their bells, and the authentic wardrobe of the participants creates an atmosphere of lighthearted nostalgia.

Joe Weinfurter, assistant to Ben Barkin, is in charge of organizing the Prelude to the Great Circus Parade. Joe and the many people that help him out do an outstanding job. The Prelude adds just the right amount of spice to get people hungry for the Circus Parade. And over the years it has grown and improved into an interesting and joyous parade in its own right.

"For at least one day every year in Milwaukee," Joe has proclaimed, "the men and women in the Prelude Parade become children again, joyfully proclaiming, 'Here Comes the Great Circus Parade!'"

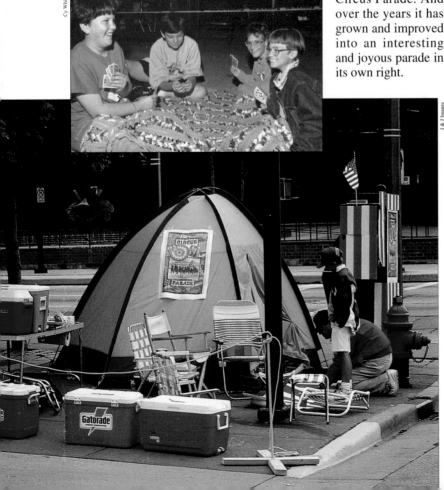

Buck Miller

Gary Bakic

Jim Morrill

Joanne K. Peterson

THE ANTIQUE CAR section of the Prelude Parade features between 35 and 40 vintage vehicles like those at left and lower left.

MILWAUKEE MAYOR John Norquist and his wife greet spectators from an antique carriage (above).

DAREDEVIL ANTICS of the high-wheel bikers, under the direction of James Fiene, offer an amusing bit of nostalgia (below).

THE AMERICAN FLAG is presented in its traditional honor with a Color Guard provided by the Milwaukee Metropolitan Non-Commissioned Officers Council.

ARM-IN-ARM. Performers on high-wheelers (above) need good balance. Beautifully restored fire equipment (right) and motorized trolley cars (below) are provided by the Milwaukee Fire Historical Society and Milwaukee Transit System. The Prelude Parade gives the city's public departments a chance to contribute to parade week.

The Wait Is Over...
'Here She Comes!'

CHAPTER TWELVE

Sitting on the grassy edge of a curb, with your feet dangling onto the street, you glance up at the hazy afternoon sun. There are people crowded all around you, including your family, but it is quiet. You hear only the sound of a far-away car and an occasional voice from the crowd.

All around the city, 750,000 or so people are waiting for the Great Circus Parade to begin—just as anxiously as you are. Getting a good viewing spot for the parade has become a ritual. Some have been in their spots for 24 hours or more. Luckily, you have a front-row seat.

"What time is it?" you almost blurt out, but decide against it. You just asked a few minutes ago. It has *got* to be near 2 o'clock. The days of waiting for the parade have been reduced to hours...now only minutes remain.

But will it ever come down the street? You watch; you wait; you listen. The sun is getting hotter. You are thirsty.

Then, ever so faintly, there is a noise in the distance. Is it a band? You look around. Nobody else seems to hear it, but now you are sure of it. It is the sound of a marching band...with horns...and cymbals. You rise to your feet and stretch your neck to look down the empty street.

At first, there is noth-

ing. Then, suddenly, you can see the colorful fluttering flags. "Here she comes!" someone cries out, and everyone stands and looks down the street.

Majestically, the mounted flag bearers of the Great Circus Parade come into

view. Oh, how those beautiful horses do prance. Now, they are right in front of you, and you smile and clap your hands to the rhythm of the band.

As a cool breeze hits your back, you know that the waiting was all worth-

TWIN LION TELESCOPING TABLEAU is pulled by eight coal-black Percherons.

Jim Morrill

HERE SHE COMES! A triumphant display of the Great Circus Parade on the first leg of its downtown tour. There are approximately 120 units in the parade, which lasts about 2-1/2 hours. A towering Uncle Sam (above right) is played by Gary Soule.

while. During the next 2 hours you will fight to slow time down, relishing every moment that flies by with the parade.

You turn to smile at your parents, but they, too, are caught up in the action. So you turn back around just in time to see a massive eight-horse hitch of shiny black Percherons coming right at you! Your heart skips a beat as they go clopping by, pulling a stunning red and gold wagon with an 18-piece band riding high on top. The "Ringling Bros. Grand Entry" is blaring. "Wow," you say under your breath.

Then you see it, the one you've been waiting for—but wait…someone once said "A picture is worth a thousand words". So take a front-row seat through the pictures on these pages. Enjoy!

THREE FAVORITE WAGONS of the parade include the Golden Age of Chivalry (top left), the Charging Tiger Tableau (middle) and the Bell Wagon (left). City Hall (above) creates a stunning backdrop for the parade.

THE TWO-HEMISPHERES BANDWAGON (above) paraded down these very streets in 1904 with the Barnum & Bailey Circus.

THREE GENERATIONS of the Sparrow family have honored the Great Circus Parade with their service. In 1972, Dick Sparrow was the first person to drive a 40-horse hitch since 1904 (upper left). His son Paul was the second, and is the current man behind the 40 (below). Paul's 14-year-old son, Jamie, drives the Wolf Tableau with his team of Roan ponies (left).

COSSACK BAND from Wauwatosa East High School, Wauwatosa, Wisconsin.

PICTURE FRAME cage wagon carries a pair of rare white tigers.

BOSTOCK AND WOMBELL BANDWAGON, built in England in 1856, is the oldest wagon in the Circus World Museum's collection of 150. About 70 of the 150 are brought for the parade.

THE COLUMBIA BANDWAGON (left) started off the wagon collection in 1957. Above: U.S. Navy Captain Kathi Dugan (in blue) is enjoying her first ride on an elephant.

ABOUT 750 HORSES participate in the Great Circus Parade! Some of the talented horse-folk wearing period costumes include King Arthur's Equestrians (top left), the Rainbow Equestriennes (above) and the lovely Ringling Equestriennes (at lower left).

PINT-SIZED HITCH (left) is comprised of 20 miniature donkeys.

RANDEM TEAM was common in the circus parades of 75 or 80 years ago. Below: Karen Schmidt rides *and* drives three horses.

Frankie B. Cole

EACH BRANCH OF THE MILITARY service is represented in the parade. Above: The U.S. Army Band of Fort Myer, Virginia.

Great Circus Parade Inc.

MATTATUCK FIFE & DRUM CORP in 1966 parade.

Frankie B. Cole

A DRUM HORSE, like one Lee Hoppe of Baraboo is riding, introduces international section of parade with rousing cadence of a kettle drum.

Jim Morrill

Kent Morrill

CHEERFUL MUSIC fills the air during the entire parade—about 30 bands and musical units march or play from atop wagons or on horseback.

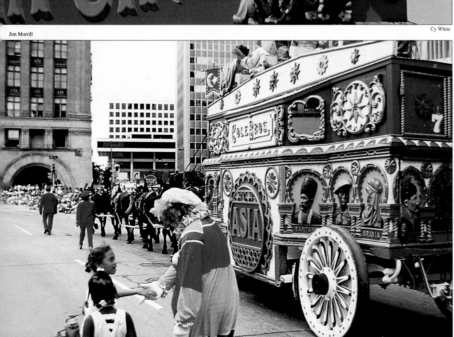

CLOWNS, CLOWNS, CLOWNS! Dr. Doolittle's Pushmi-Pullyu is an old-time "two-headed horse" clown gag from the Ringling Bros. adaptation of the land of Pudleby. Below: A high-class clown, Walter "never falter" Jankowski, greets a little fan.

ERNIE BORGNINE has been popular at the parade since 1970. At left: Chief clown Art Petrie rides in a clown cart.

TWO JOLLY ELEPHANTS from the Circus World Museum had to practice daily to prepare for this parade chore. Wagon 116 contains a melodious air calliope. Lou Jacobs (below left), a 50-year veteran from the Ringling Bros. Circus, is one of the most famous clowns in circus history. The one-horsepower automobile (below right) is another ancient clown gag the audience enjoys.

TU-TALL, the Circus World Museum's resident giraffe, views the city through his replicated giraffe den from the 1893 Ringling Bros. Circus.

THE KING of the (parade) jungle!

EIGHT-CAMEL HITCH pulls "Cleopatra" aboard the Temple Tableau.

PLAYFUL BEAR CUBS are active along the entire parade route.

THE HIPPO (above) enjoys the parade so long as he is with his friends—the elephants. Old circuses used to advertise "Lion loose in the streets!" to draw people to their parades. Actually, these cats are quite docile. Above right, a cheetah enjoys his view of the 1969 parade. Below, a tethered leopard paces aboard the Temple Tableau.

MRS. HENRY RINGLING JR., the daughter-in-law of the great showman, represents the legendary Ringling family in the parade.

SIGNS OF APPRECIATION from spectators appear all along the parade route.

THE 50 STATE FLAG UNIT from the Great Lakes Naval Training Station in Illinois shows us that this truly is *America's* Great Circus Parade.

20 AFRICAN AND ASIAN ELEPHANTS (center right) shake the earth as they shuffle through the parade every year.

MERRY MUSIC of the America Steam Calliope (right) signals the end of the parade. See you next year!

'Oh, to Ride in the Great Circus Parade!'

The first Great Circus Parade took place on July 4, 1963. The Schlitz Brewery sponsored the parade in those days, and did so through 1973. During this period I was both the director of the Circus World Musuem and the director of the parade.

Needless to say, on parade day, I was busier than a one-armed billposter on a windy day. This day of organized confusion made it hard to even blink an eye without missing something—horses, wagons, bands, equestrians, tigers, lions, hippos, camels and elephants all had to get organized and out on the street in good order.

Even though I was so busy, I must confess that on occasion, I caught myself dreaming. The dream was to *ride* in the Great Circus Parade. Ten feet up, on a huge bandwagon adorned with wood carvings—emblazoned with brilliant colors and waving banners.

It was a dream that I turned to again and again, but usually shrugged off be-cause I knew I was needed elsewhere.

The parade was discontinued in 1973, after I retired. But in 1985, through Ben Barkin's foresight, diligence and love for Milwaukee, the Great Circus Parade was revived.

I was assigned the job of narrating the local TV coverage of the parade. The toughest part of that task was sitting with my back to the parade and watching the TV monitor. I wanted to see the real thing!

One of the broadcasters I was work-

Jim Morrill

A NEW PERSPECTIVE! Chappie rides in his first Great Circus Parade. After directing the parade for 10 years, and supplying TV commentary for 5, he finally got to see the parade from a different angle in 1990.

Jim Morrill

"TAKE THE LINES, MY ARMS ARE TIRED," Dick Sparrow (center) said to Chappie (right). "Before I realized what was happening, I was driving the team—or at least pretending to do so," said Chappie. That's the brakeman, Lester Hindeman, on the left.

ing with would keep nudging me and saying, "Talk about what you see on the *monitor*." It was a pain in the neck, literally, as I kept unconsciously twisting around to see the teams and wagons.

I continued with this task through 1989. In 1990 I didn't receive an invi-

---

"If you are not tied up tomorrow I have a spot on my wagon for you."
Kaboom—my dream had come true!

---

tation. I guess I must have messed up so badly that the television crew ran out of patience. I do not blame them one little bit.

Then, on the day before the 1990 Great Circus Parade, a misunderstanding left an 18-piece band with no wagon to ride in. Greg Parkinson, director of the museum, acted fast and had a spare bandwagon trucked in from Baraboo.

Greg then went to see Dick Sparrow, whose son Paul was driving the 40-horse hitch, and asked if he could put together a six-horse hitch with his spare horses.

Later on that day, Dick stopped by the press tent where I was parked. "If you are not tied up tomorrow, I have a spot on my wagon for you."

K a b o o m — m y dream had come true! It took me all of 2 seconds to say yes.

That Saturday afternoon, driving to the hotel, I was astonished to see scores of people camped out along the curbs of the parade route—it would be a 20-hour wait! My mind flashed back to 1962 when we were trying to find a sponsor.

I would make extravagant statements like, "There will be thousands of people jammed downtown to see the parade." I am glad that I did not get carried away and say, "Mr. Barkin, people will be camping out a day ahead of time just to get a good spot." That might have squelched Ben's interest. He is imaginative, but not gullible.

My invitation to ride in the Great

JAKE POSEY drove the 40-horse hitch for Barnum & Bailey in Europe at the turn of the century. Later, he was "Boss Hostler" in Buffalo Bill's Wild West Show.

A HORSEMAN'S VIEW. In 1991, the author received another opportunity to ride in the parade—only this time with Paul Sparrow, aboard the Two-Hemispheres Bandwagon behind 40 Belgians.

Jim Morrill

HEARTY HANDSHAKE and word of thanks to Paul Sparrow for the experience of being his brakeman aboard the famous 40-horse hitch.

Circus Parade came so unexpectedly that it was difficult to fall asleep Saturday night. I began to think about all of the magnificent parade wagons I had collected for the Circus World Museum during the '60s.

These glorious wagons had been built 80, 90, 100 and more years ago for the greatest circus men who ever lived: Adam Forepaugh, Barnum & Bailey, the Ringlings, Charley Sparks, the Gollmars and others. Having paraded down the main streets of cities and towns all over the country, the wagons were like old friends to Americans.

The next day, I arrived at the show grounds early and reported to Dick Sparrow's tent. Our six Belgians were harnessed and then led over to our assigned wagon, the Lion and Gladiator. A glorious bandwagon from the Hagenbeck-Wallace Circus, it was painted red and featured stunning gold carvings of a Roman Gladiator wrestling a lion.

The musicians climbed aboard, then Dick Sparrow was seated. On his right was the brakeman, Lester Hindeman, Dick's longtime friend and partner.

Yours truly climbed aboard and sat on Dick's left. I felt like excess baggage, but was darned excited to see the Great Circus Parade from a different angle. I was about to find out that the top of a wagon beats any view of the parade in the city.

Dick called "Hi-ya!" to the team, and onto the parade route we went. I could see an ocean of people for blocks and blocks, everybody clapping, whistling and cheering…I got a little choked up. These ancient wagons were rolling down the street, entertaining the townsfolk just as they were designed to do a century ago.

As we rounded a corner and headed west, Dick said, without notice, "Here,

---

"I could see an ocean of people for blocks and blocks, everybody clapping, whistling and cheering…I got a little choked up…"

Fox, take the lines. My arms are tired." Before I knew it, I was driving the team! I held the lines for about a block or two—and what a sensation.

In those two blocks, I felt a great deal of respect and admiration for all the horsemen in our parade. I had never realized how much pride they must take in their work—the strength and savvy required to master this age-old profession.

When the parade was over, I was exhilarated. I felt 20 years younger.

Riding in the Great Circus Parade was an experience that I savored all fall, winter and into the spring of 1991.

Then the phone rang. It was Paul Sparrow, calling from Zearing, Iowa to invite me to be his brakeman aboard the 40-horse hitch in the upcoming parade!

It was hard for me to believe I would have this experience. I had written about the old 40-horse hitches of circus fame and researched the Two-Hemispheres Bandwagon extensively. Built in 1903 for Barnum & Bailey, it is the largest parade wagon ever—28 feet long and weighs almost 8 tons.

I also knew that this wagon paraded down Wisconsin Avenue in Milwaukee in 1904—the very last year a 40-horse hitch appeared in parade. Paul had given me the opportunity of a lifetime, and this I relished right up to the moment the parade started at 2 o'clock.

At that point, all the excitement and emotion were forgotten, and it was all business. Braking the wagon involves turning a wheel that in turn clamps brake shoes to the rear wheels of the wagon.

Saluting Ben Barkin

A few weeks before the parade, Ben Barkin's publicity department sent a release to TV stations and newspapers. It said that I would be riding as brakeman on the 40-horse hitch wagon and that I'd be wearing my brown felt hat instead of a pith helmet. Well, I thought, I am not going to be the first one to break my own rules.

But I decided to play the gag on Ben Barkin: When we got to the reviewing stand where Ben was stationed, I reached for my fedora and put it on top of my pith helmet, and kept it there for about 30 seconds, acting like nothing was out of the ordinary.

When Ben glanced over at me, he burst into a loud laugh—so I forgave myself for breaking the wardrobe regulations.

Our unit was called into the parade line at 3:35 p.m. Paul shouted, "Outriders ready?" and six right hands shot up in the air signaling all okay. "Move 'er out!" he shouted. And with whistles and calls to the team, he had all 40 Belgians moving beautifully.

A few blocks into the parade, we came to the reviewing stand and Paul brought the team to a stop. Then, to the amazement of all, he backed the 40 horses 20 feet. The applause was thunderous. It was the only bit of funning on the entire parade route, and it was done for the benefit of

BREAKING THE RULES? Just for fun, Chappie donned his trusty fedora over required pith helmet before riding on wagon behind 40-horse hitch (below) in 1991.

Ben Barkin, who masterminds the fund-raising necessary to stage this great event. Such beautiful teamwork!

Paul's superb team was performing one of the most difficult feats of horsemanship ever seen—and they made it look easy. But the tens of thousands of people loved the show. There was a standing ovation as we moved down the streets. This appreciation was heartwarming and so very rewarding.

At 5 o'clock, the 40 rolled back onto the show grounds. We had been out on the Milwaukee streets for 1-1/2 hours, but I could swear it was only 20 minutes. It was an experience that I will never forget.

In the nearly 20 years that the Great Circus Parade has been going, I have had some pretty wonderful experiences. From walking into Ben Barkin's office in 1963 with a handful of old photos, to riding down the streets of Milwaukee behind the 40-horse hitch in 1991, I feel truly fortunate to have been involved with such a wonderful event.

*P*lease Accept Our Heartfelt Thanks...

THERE ARE HUNDREDS of great photographs in this book, spanning the history of the Great Circus Parade, which was held annually from 1963 through 1973, then started up again in 1985 and has been held every year since. To all of the photographers whose magnificent photos appear in these pages, we offer our sincere thanks for sharing your work. The following is a list of the men and women who have captured and preserved the magic of the Great Circus Parade with their beautiful images over the years:

John Ahlhauser, Ernie Anheuser, Richard Bauer, Garry Bakic, Frankie B. Cole, James Conklin, Nancy Cutlip, Don Emmerich, Sherman Gessert, Arnie Gore, Sam Koshollek, Henry Larsen, Paul Larson, Neils Lauritzen, Joy Lewis, Angus McDougall, Buck Miller, Jim Morrill, Kent Morrill, John Murray, Don Nusbaum, Joanne Peterson, Frank Scherschel, Clarence Schmidt, Allan Scott, James Stanfield, Fred Tonne, Chris Wheeler, Cy White and John Zweifel.

We would also like to extend our appreciation to all of the businesses, public departments and volunteers who have helped us out; and most importantly, to the thousands of fans who show up to cheer the Great Circus Parade on every year. You are all "Center Ring" performers!

Chappie Fox